Take the quiz
then test y

1. General Robert E. Lee's father was Henry Lee, "Light-Horse Harry," a general in the American Revolution.
2. The famous ship that changed the course of naval warfare, signaling the end of wooden warships, was built in Brooklyn, New York.
3. General Winfield Scott, a hero of the Mexican War.
4. From July 13 to July 16, 1863, almost one thousand civilians were killed and wounded in one of the worst draft riots in American history. It took place in New York City.
5. The commander of the Union forces in the West, John C. Fremont, named Ulysses Grant to command an important post at Cairo, Illinois at the beginning of the war.
6. Vice President Andrew Johnson and Secretary of State William Seward.
7. Union General George Brinton McClellan.
8. The submarine was the Confederate *Hunley*, and it sank the Union warship *Housatonic*.
9. Though the name of the battle is never mentioned in the novel, the accounts of the actual fighting most closely resemble Chancellorsville, May 2–4, 1863.
10. The man often credited with the founding of baseball, Abner Doubleday was also a Union general who fought at the Battle of Gettysburg.

The
CIVIL WAR
Trivia Quiz
Book

★ ★ ★ ★ ★ ★

William Terdoslavich

WARNER BOOKS

A Warner Communications Company

WARNER BOOKS EDITION

Copyright © 1984 by William Terdoslavich

Cover design by Gene Light
Cover art by Jim Dietz

Warner Books, Inc.
666 Fifth Avenue
New York, N.Y. 10103

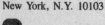 A Warner Communications Company

Printed in the United States of America

First Printing: November, 1984

10 9 8 7 6 5 4 3 2 1

For Donna
Thank you for your help and understanding.
Thank you for being there.

ACKNOWLEDGMENTS

I would like to thank Brian Thomsen of Warner Books and Donna Benedetto, a woman who is very near and dear to me, for their help with this book.

Contents

Introduction

The Civil War was the bloodiest war ever fought in American history. For a brief time, the armies of the Union and the Confederacy numbered as great as those of the European powers. The military task facing the Union was equally as great, since the southern states that had to be conquered had a land area roughly comparable to Europe.

Like all wars, there were certain elements still in the embryonic stage that were to evolve into deadlier weapons in later wars. The observation balloon, the submarine, the machine gun, and the turreted battleship all had forebears in this conflict.

With the invention of the telegraph and the railroad, armies could remain supplied for long periods in the field while staying in touch with distant commanders and political leaders. But one of the biggest changes was the fact that the Civil War was the first truly total war of the industrial age.

Because of this, economic strength mattered just as much as generalship. The North survived a string of inept commanders that would have resulted in the defeat of other nations in earlier days. At the same time, a string of brilliant generals did not add up to victory for the South. The war was decided by numbers, not by daring strokes and brilliant moves.

But it is the daring strokes and the brilliant moves that arouse the interest of those who read about the war. The economic factors underly the war but aren't so dramatic or so apparent as the battles and the campaigns. Union musket production just doesn't rank up there in imagery with the "High-Water Mark of the Confederacy" at Gettysburg.

While it is easy to take in the more colorful picture of the war, which exists with Robert E. Lee and the exploits of the Army of Northern Virginia, one must remember that the war was won in the West, not the East. The loss of Richmond would have been more of a psychological blow for the Confederacy, had it occurred earlier. Another capital would have been found for the government. But the loss of Vicksburg was mortal. For the South, it was passage past the economic point of no return.

Personalities also make the war an engrossing subject to study. Aside from being a daring commander and bold strategist, Robert E. Lee was loved by his men to the point of devotion. Ulysses S. Grant was more of an oddball. Even though he was a general in command of an army, at Shiloh most of his men didn't even recognize him. In civilian life, he was less than a success, but the war brought him to the forefront.

Other figures seem more human when one looks at what they did before the war. Abraham Lincoln, for example, once had a woman turn down his proposal for marriage. Philip Sheridan had a quick temper that nearly got him thrown out of West Point. A. P. Hill and George McClellan once competed for the hand of the same woman. And one former vice-president took up arms against the Union as a Confederate general. (To find out who, read on.)

This book is a mixture of history and trivia about the war. Die-hard Civil War buffs may be disappointed that their favorite piece of obscure knowledge may not be included. But you can only cover so much in a thousand questions. What you will find between these covers is a delicate balance between the important events of the war that are barely mentioned in school history books, and such stuff as will sorely test the brains of those obsessed with trivial pursuits.

The Civil War did not start overnight. The issue of slavery had festered politically since the beginning of the nineteenth century, amid much legislative wrangling and a landmark Supreme Court case.

★ ★ ★

What Led to the War

1. In the 1840s, how much money was invested in slaves in the South?

2. In 1860, how many of the South's white population owned slaves?

3. In 1831, a self-educated slave sparked a slave rebellion in Southampton County, Virginia. Who was he?

4. What southern state tried previously to secede and why?

5. How was this previous secession attempt handled by President Andrew Jackson?

6. What was the Missouri Compromise? When was it passed?

7. Where was the "demarcation line" between slave and free states?

8. How many copies of *Uncle Tom's Cabin* were sold during its first year of publication?

9. What act was targeted for repeal by popular sentiment following the book's success?

10. What change in the procedure for admitting states as "slave" or "free" was introduced in Congress in 1854? Who was the senator who introduced it?

11. What were "Bushwackers" and "Jayhawkers"?

12. What territory suffered a violent influx of those two groups seeking to establish residency?

13. What was the territory nicknamed because of the violence?

14. Noted abolitionist John Brown led a massacre of pro-slavery people in Kansas. Where?

15. In 1857, a slave belonging to an army surgeon sued for his freedom when he accompanied his master to Minnesota. Who was the slave?

16. What was his argument?

17. Who wrote the Supreme Court decision for this case?

18. What was the Court's decision?

19. Who were the two justices who dissented in this case?

20. How was the case a victory for the slave states?

21. In 1858, a senate-seat debate in Illinois received national attention. Who were the participants?

22. What political effect did the debate have on one of these participants?

23. In October 1857, John Brown went to which state to start a slave insurrection?

24. What happened to Brown after he seized the Union arsenal at Harpers Ferry?

25. A unit of the Virginia Militia was guarding the execution yard where Brown was eventually hanged. A young private in that unit would gain notoriety shortly after the war ended. Who was he?

The Civil War was more than just a series of battles. Both sides drew strength from their industrial bases, and a measure of this capability was just as important as their troops in the field.

Statistics

1. Which was the most populous Union state?

2. Which Union state was the least populous?

3. Which state was the most populous in the Confederacy?

4. Which Confederate state was the least populous?

5. Which southern state had the largest slave population?

6. Which northern state had the greatest number of businesses?

7. Which southern state was the Confederacy's industrial leader?

8. What was the total number of Union enlistments in the war (approximately)?

9. What was the total number of Confederate enlistments during the war (approximately)?

10. How many men were killed on both sides during the war (approximately)?

Behind every general, regardless of whether he was talented, were his troops. While the big battles and events of the war are standard reading in any history book, the everyday life of the soldier is sometimes overlooked.

Union Soldiers

1. Were officers given rations or allowances in the Union Army?

2. Name the standard biscuit ration made of flour and water.

3. What was a "Jonah"?

4. What was a "beat"?

5. What was a "housewife"?

6. What was the "black list"? What was it used for?

7. What was a "bounty jumper"?

8. What was "hay foot" and "straw foot"?

9. What was a "sutler"?

10. What was a "havelock"?

Confederate Soldiers

1. What was "slosh" or "coosh"?

2. What was the most common profession among southern soldiers?

3. What kind of game was "hot jackets"?

4. What did rebels use for a ball to play "tenpins"?

5. What was "gander pulling"?

6. What was "fox and geese"?

7. What was a "barrel shirt"?

8. What was another name for the latrine?

9. What was the most common disease among southern soldiers?

10. For diarrhea or malaria, what was the rebel field cure?

The Civil War also saw some advances in weapons technology which would lead to greater bloodshed in future wars.

Weapons

1. Muskets in the Revolutionary War and the War of 1812 were called "flintlocks" because the hammer had a piece of flint which caused the spark needed to fire the gun. By the time of the Civil War, flintlocks were no longer widely used. What was used to cause the spark on most Civil War rifles?

2. Old flintlocks were "smoothbore" muskets, but Civil War muskets were rifled. What effect did this have on the guns?

3. The Civil War musket didn't fire a round lead ball. What did it fire and what did it look like?

4. This breech-loading carbine was widely used by the cavalry in the Civil War. Name it.

5. The first successful repeating rifle ever made was used by the Union army. A brigade of Michigan cavalry under Custer used it at Gettysburg. Name it.

6. During Sherman's March to the Sea, two regiments under Major General Dodge were armed with a unique repeating rifle. Name it.

7. Over two hundred thousand .44-caliber revolvers of this type were made and used in the Civil War. Name it.

8. Modern revolvers fire metallic cartridges. How did this revolver differ in this respect?

9. This gun mounted twenty-five barrels on a carriage and was fired by striking a single percussion cap which ignited a common train of powder. Name it.

10. This crude machine gun had one barrel, and bullets were fired by being poured into a hopper on its top. Name it.

11. Used at the Battle of Seven Pines, Virginia, this Confederate machine gun was mounted on a carriage and fired paper cartridges. Name it.

12. This six-barreled machine gun was invented by a physician who took a greater interest in mechanical inventions than in medicine. Name it.

13. What reason did the Union give for not purchasing this weapon for use in the Civil War?

14. The first Gatling Guns produced were of what caliber?

15. How many bullets does a Spencer Carbine hold?

16. Where did a Spencer store its bullets?

17. The Confederacy only had two of these long-range cannon at the Battle of Gettysburg. Name them.

18. About 428,000 of these English muzzle-loaders were purchased for use in the Civil War. Name them and their caliber.

19. What was a "Quaker gun"? Where were they used and why?

20. What special type of shot was used by artillery at close range to stop an infantry attack? What was it made of?

There were some units during the war that were elite and had colorful histories. How many of them do you know?

Regiments and Units

1. What was the nickname of the Union's First Brigade, First Division, I Corps?

2. What regiments made up the First Brigade, First Division, I Corps?

3. What was the designation of the Orphan Brigade? Which army did it fight for?

4. Name the regiments that formed the Orphan Brigade.

5. Brevet Brigadier General Custer commanded what brigades before Gettysburg? Name the regiments.

6. What two additions were made to the brigade before Custer left command?

7. What type of regiment was the 1st District of Columbia?

8. What type of officers did the Union assign to the newly formed West Virginia units?

9. Col. Charles Rainsford Jennison raised what regiment during pre–Civil War unrest in Kansas?

10. What was the official designation of Jennison's regiment? What was its nickname?

11. What regiments made up the "Stonewall Brigade"?

The presidential election year saw the emergence of the Republican Party, and the division of the Democratic Party along regional lines. Politically chaotic, this year saw four men running for president.

Politics of 1860

1. In February 1860, Lincoln was invited by New York City Republicans to deliver a speech. Where?

2. The Republican Convention was held in what city? What was the name of the convention hall?

3. In what city was the Democratic Convention held?

4. How many ballots did it take to nominate Lincoln?

5. Who was the favored candidate at the Republican Convention?

6. How many ballots were cast at the Democratic Convention? What was the result?

7. When the Democratic Party reconvened its convention in Baltimore, whom did they pick as candidate and running mate?

8. Southern seceders, calling themselves the National Democratic Party, also met in Baltimore. Whom did they nominate for president and vice-president?

9. When Fitzpatrick withdrew, whom did the National Committee pick as Douglas's running mate?

10. The Constitutional Union Party was made up of remnants from which party? In which states was it strongest?

11. Whom did the Constitutional Party nominate for president and vice-president?

12. In what order did the candidates finish in a popular vote? How many votes did each candidate get?

13. In what order did the candidates finish in electoral votes? How many electoral votes did each candidate get?

14. Douglas, who was senator from Illinois, won one state and a partial vote from another. Name them.

15. Who were the "Wide-Awakes"?

16. In the Republican platform of 1860, was Congress supposed to have freedom in deciding if slavery could be legalized in certain territories?

17. When the seceded states in 1861 went about choosing a president, how many states were there? How many delegates?

18. How were the votes apportioned?

19. Who was a leading contender for the Confederate presidency before the convention picked Jefferson Davis?

20. Where did this convention gather?

21. How long was the president's term under the Confederate Constitution?

22. Did the Confederate Constitution have any language about the right of a state to secede?

23. Were protective tariffs allowed by the Confederate Constitution?

24. What unique veto power was given to the Confederate president?

25. What type of majority did the Confederate Congress need to appropriate money?

The Civil War made the leaders of both sides appear larger than life. But as the following section shows, they were in some cases very ordinary. Who would guess that an obscure Illinois lawyer would eventually preside over the nation in its greatest crisis? How were the Union generals in the war's early days to know that an obscure Illinois brigadier would later be instrumental in winning the war?

Abraham Lincoln (1809–1865)

1. In what county and state was Lincoln born?

2. How old was Lincoln when his family moved and where did they go?

3. Give the names of Lincoln's natural mother and his stepmother.

4. What was the first law book read by Lincoln?

5. In what military action did Lincoln first gain experience?

6. To what rank was he elected?

7. What rank did Lincoln hold when he reenlisted for a third time during this action, and for how long was his enlistment?

8. What was the first political office Lincoln sought, and for what party?

9. Where in Illinois did Lincoln first settle?

10. How well did Lincoln fare in his first election, and how many votes did he get?

11. Lincoln borrowed law books from a fellow veteran of the Black Hawk War who was practicing law in Springfield. Name him.

12. When was Lincoln finally elected to the state legislature?

13. Name the first woman Lincoln courted. What happened to her?

14. Who was the second woman Lincoln tried to court? What happened when he proposed?

15. What was the nature of the first piece of legislation Lincoln introduced in the legislature, and what happened to it?

16. To what committee in the state legislature was Lincoln assigned?

17. When Lincoln became licensed to practice law in 1837, with whom did he become partners?

18. Lincoln eventually became engaged to Mary Todd. Who else competed for her hand in marriage?

19. What happened to Mary Todd on her wedding day in 1841?

20. In 1844, Lincoln became an elector for what presidential candidate? Did the candidate win?

21. In 1846, Lincoln was elected to a higher political office. What was it? What distinction did he hold?

22. How long did Lincoln's congressional career last?

23. President-elect Zachary Taylor offered Lincoln a territorial post, which would have given him a chance of being elected senator once that territory was admitted into the United States. What territory was it, and what was Lincoln's decision?

24. In 1855, Lincoln ran for the post of U.S. Senator from Illinois. Whom did the state legislature elect?

25. When the Whig Party broke up in 1856, Lincoln had to politically realign himself. There were three parties he could have chosen. Name them. Which one did he choose?

Jefferson Davis (1808–1889)

1. What war did Jefferson Davis's father fight in?

2. In what county and state was Davis born? What was notable about the location?

3. When Davis turned eight, his father sent him to school in Mississippi. Name the school. What made Davis's presence unusual there?

4. Davis entered the military academy at West Point in 1824. In his first year at the academy, what was he brought up on charges for?

5. In 1826, Cadet Davis was again brought up on charges by Academy authorities. What did he do this time?

6. When Davis was graduated from West Point, what was his class standing?

7. While assigned to Fort Crawford as a lieutenant, Davis fell in love with the daughter of his commanding officer. Who was Davis's commanding officer? What was the name of his daughter?

8. In 1838, Maj. R. B. Mason brought charges against Davis. For what was Davis court-martialed? What event led to this?

9. What was Davis's defense at his court-martial? What was the verdict?

10. Why did Davis resign from the army in 1835?

11. Three months after Davis was married, what happened?

12. After eight years as a plantation owner, Davis met his second wife. What was her name?

13. What was the name of Davis's plantation?

14. To what party did Davis belong, and when and how did he first get involved in politics?

15. As a result of the convention, for what office was Davis nominated? What happened?

16. In 1845, to what office was Davis elected?

17. Within two weeks of arriving in Washington, Davis made his first speech in the House of Representatives. What was he taking a stand on?

18. When the Mexican War broke out, what was Davis's position on it?

19. What rule in Congress did Davis break with his speeches in his first term?

20. Mississippi was only allowed to raise one regiment to contribute to President Polk's call for fifty thousand volunteers. What was the name of the regiment? What rank did Davis hold in it?

21. Under what general did Davis serve in the Mexican War?

22. At what battle did Davis distinguish himself?

23. In 1847, Davis returned to Washington, elected to what office?

24. What committee did he chair?

25. In 1851, Davis lost the election for governor in Mississippi. He was temporarily retired from politics until Franklin Pierce became president in 1853. What Cabinet post did Davis accept in the Pierce Administration?

Ulysses S. Grant (1822–1885)

1. What was Grant's full name?

2. In what area was Grant to show an early talent?

3. How old was Grant when he entered West Point and what year was that in?

4. What rank did Grant hold in his second year at West Point?

5. In what place did Grant graduate?

6. To what unit was he first assigned as a second lieutenant?

7. Where did Grant first see action in the Mexican War?

8. Under what general did Grant's unit first fight?

9. When Grant was transferred along with some of Taylor's units to Vera Cruz to serve under Winfield Scott, what unit was he with?

10. What position did he hold in that regiment?

11. In what battle were Grant's actions cited in dispatches?

12. Where was Grant stationed after the Mexican War?

13. Whom did Grant marry?

14. When did Grant resign from the army?

15. What did Grant do when he went to Galena, Illinois?

16. To what regiment was Grant assigned and with what rank when the Civil War broke out?

17. What role did Rep. Elihu P. Washburne play in Grant's military career?

18. Union Gen. John C. Fremont appointed Grant to which important outpost?

19. What nickname was given to Grant after the surrender of Forts Henry and Donelson?

20. Who ran against Grant for president in 1868?

21. In 1880, when Grant was being considered by the Republicans for the nomination for a third term as president, who beat Grant to the nomination?

22. Name the brokerage firm that Grant founded in New York which later failed.

23. How much money did Grant's memoirs earn?

24. What rank was conferred upon Grant by Congress after the war, and why was it significant?

25. What rank was conferred upon Grant by Abraham Lincoln in order to make him supreme commander of all Union forces?

Robert E. Lee (1807–1870)

1. In what war did Robert E. Lee's father fight?

2. What graduating class did Lee belong to at West Point?

3. Lee was one of four Virginians who enrolled in West Point in 1825. Two of them would drop out by graduation. Who was the other Virginian in Lee's class?

4. In what place did Lee graduate in his West Point class?

5. To what army general did Lee become a trusted adviser in the Mexican War?

6. Lee became a guide for a division in a battle that was the key to taking Mexico City. Which battle was that?

7. What rank did Lee start at in the Mexican War? What rank did he attain?

8. In 1852, Colonel Lee received one of the army's best assignments. What was it?

9. Whom did Lee marrry in 1831?

10. Lee had a nephew who entered West Point in 1852, and was twice nearly expelled for sneaking off the

grounds at night to visit a nearby tavern. Who was he, and what would he later become?

11. In 1855, two new cavalry regiments were raised. To which regiment was Lee assigned, with what rank, and under whom did he serve?

12. What was Lee's position on slavery before the Civil War?

13. In late 1859, Lee was ordered to put down a slave insurrection. Where was it?

14. In March 1861, Lee was offered positions in both the Union and Confederate armies. What ranks did the Union and Confederacy offer him?

15. The Union later made a greater offer which he refused. What was it?

16. What was Lee's first Confederate appointment?

17. What was Lee's first rank in the regular Confederate Army?

18. What theater of operations was first given to Lee? How long did he command there?

19. What incident prompted President Jefferson Davis to appoint Lee to command the Army of Northern Virginia?

20. What nickname was given to Lee by his men, and what did it mean?

21. What was the name of Lee's horse?

22. In 1865, Lee supported a new policy that would lend

support to the South's declining manpower. What was that policy?

23. Where did Lee settle shortly after the war's end?

24. In June 1865, Lee wrote a letter to President Andrew Johnson. What was he writing for?

25. What position did Lee assume after the war?

Braxton Bragg (1817–1876)

1. When did Bragg graduate from West Point?

2. What was his rank when he was with the 3rd Artillery?

3. In what war did he see his first military action?

4. Under what general did he serve in the Mexican War?

5. At what battle did he distinguish himself?

6. At the Battle of Buena Vista, General Taylor rode up to Bragg's battery and issued a famous order. What was it?

7. What brevet rank did he achieve?

8. In Mexico, what hazardous action *off* the battlefield did Bragg encounter?

9. What future Confederate general accompanied him on an expedition to Utah?

10. On January 3, 1856, what did Bragg do that was significant in his career?

11. What post was Bragg given when the Civil War began?

12. What post and rank was he given afterward by President Jefferson Davis?

13. While holding this command, he made a night attack on which Union-held island?

14. When Bragg was pulled from field command, what was his post?

15. What was Bragg's last field command?

16. Bragg was a stern disciplinarian. How did he treat desertion?

17. Bragg once had three soldiers executed for what offense?

18. What did Bragg do after the Civil War?

19. At Kinston in 1865, Bragg attacked a Union column. How many prisoners did he take?

20. How was Bragg popularly known?

Thomas "Stonewall" Jackson (1824–1863)

1. In 1842, an event occurred that changed Jackson's life. What was it?

2. In his plebe year at West Point, what group did Jackson fall in with?

3. Jackson was graduated from West Point in 1846 in a class of 60. In what subject was his lowest standing?

4. When Jackson returned to his hometown a few days before leaving for the Mexican War, he accepted an invitation from Colonel McKinley to drill a company of the local militia. What happened?

5. To what unit was Jackson first assigned?

6. What was Jackson's first action of the Mexican War?

7. When the American army was storming Chapultepec, Jackson refused to obey the order of a superior officer. What was that order?

8. When Mexican troops fled Chapultepec, what did Jackson and his commanding officer do?

9. To what rank was Jackson promoted after Chapultepec?

10. In 1851, Jackson drew an academic assignment to which school?

11. What was his post at that school?

12. Jackson made a modest business investment after returning to Virginia. What was it?

13. What was Jackson's nickname at the Virginia Military Institute?

14. VMI commandant Colonel Francis Smith one day called Jackson to his office and asked him to wait in the

anteroom. While Smith attended to other business, he forgot about Jackson. What happened to Jackson? What did Jackson say about this little slip-up?

15. In 1854, Jackson was turned down for a professorship. By what school? For what subject? Whose recommendation did he have?

16. In November 1854, Jackson's wife died. How?

17. When the Civil War broke out, what was Jackson ordered to do?

18. What was Jackson's rank shortly after the war began? Where was he first sent?

19. Who relieved Jackson at Harpers Ferry?

20. At what battle did Jackson earn his nickname "Stonewall"?

George McClellan (1826–1885)

1. What year did McClellan enter West Point?

2. What city was McClellan born in?

3. A regulation was waived to allow McClellan to enter West Point. What was it?

4. What future generals did McClellan count as his classmates at West Point?

5. What was McClellan's class-standing when he was graduated?

6. What was McClellan's first rank?

7. As an engineer, what siege did McClellan participate in during the Mexican War?

8. What happened to McClellan at the Battle of Contreras?

9. What brevet rank was awarded to McClellan after Chapultepec?

10. In 1849, a study board was formed to look at the campaigns of a famous European general. Who was that general? Which of his campaigns did McClellan study?

11. What future general and former classmate beat McClellan out to an appointment to VMI?

12. In 1852, McClellan was part of an expedition under Capt. Randolph Marcy. What was the expedition's purpose?

13. Whom did McClellan marry?

14. When Congress raised four new cavalry regiments, to which one was McClellan assigned? With what rank?

15. What was McClellan sent to observe in 1855?

16. What civilian job did McClellan accept in 1857?

17. What lawyer did McClellan meet during this time who would later become politically prominent?

18. What position did McClellan attain in his civilian job in 1858?

19. Who was McClellan's roommate at West Point?

20. McClellan's wife broke an engagement to marry McClellan. Whom did she jilt?

John Singleton Mosby (1833–1916)

1. What was Mosby's profession before the war?

2. What were his sentiments at the war's beginning?

3. What Confederate volunteer cavalry unit did Mosby join?

4. What was Mosby's rank?

5. When Mosby was 16, what university was he sent to?

6. In his third year at the university, Mosby was arrested. What for?

7. How did Mosby get out of jail after serving most of his one-year sentence?

8. Who was the prosecutor that locked up Mosby and later became his legal mentor?

9. Under what Confederate cavalry commander did Mosby first serve?

10. On his way to Stonewall Jackson in 1862, Mosby was captured by Union cavalry. What regiment captured him?

11. What wound did Mosby suffer at Second Manassas?

12. What Union general did Mosby kidnap from the large Union encampment at Fairfax Courthouse?

13. The Stoughton kidnapping earned what rank for Mosby?

14. What British captain served in Mosby's unit?

15. What state provided a large number of men for Mosby's cavalry unit and why?

16. What motive was there for joining Mosby's unit?

17. What Confederate law made legal the exploits of Mosby and other freebooting units?

18. What Union cavalry unit was the first to rout Mosby?

19. When Mosby finally had enough men enrolled in his unit, what designation was it given when it was officially sworn into the Confederate Army?

20. Whom did Mosby kidnap in September 1863 from Alexandria, Virginia, and what was his position?

William T. Sherman (1820–1891)

1. What was Sherman's nickname? How did it come about?

2. When did Sherman receive his appointment to West Point?

3. At West Point, what was "Benny Haven's" noted for? What relation did Sherman have with it? Because of it, what reputation did Sherman establish for himself at West Point?

4. What was Sherman's first assignment? What action did his unit see?

5. What was Sherman's class standing when he was graduated from West Point?

6. When Sherman was at Fort Pierce, an assault was made on the Seminole Indians which was the first military action Sherman took part in. What role did he play?

7. After seventeen months of service, Sherman received something that usually took five years to obtain. What was it?

8. After the Seminole War ended, where was Sherman assigned?

9. Where was Sherman when the Mexican War broke out in 1846?

10. Sherman was sent where during the Mexican War?

11. What action did Sherman see during the Mexican War?

12. What significant event in 1848 did Sherman witness in Northern California?

13. Sherman made a small fortune at this time doing what?

14. Whom did Sherman marry, and what was notable about her?

15. The woman Sherman married was Catholic. What was his religion?

16. After a six-month leave in Washington in 1850, Sherman received a new assignment. To what unit was he assigned? Who was his commanding officer?

17. Shortly after this assignment, Sherman was promoted to captain. To what branch of service was he assigned?

18. Sherman went to San Francisco for a six-month leave to try his hand at a different profession. What was it? What firm did he work for?

19. What was "The Battle of 23 February?"

20. What was Sherman's post when the southern states began seceding?

"Jeb" Stuart (1833–1864)

1. What did "Jeb" stand for?

2. In what war did Stuart's father fight?

3. What was Stuart's class standing when he was graduated from West Point in 1854?

4. What was the highest cavalry rank Stuart held as a cadet?

5. What kind of regiment was Stuart first assigned to? With what rank?

6. When Congress raised new cavalry regiments in 1855, to which one was Stuart assigned and with what rank?

7. In 1856, Stuart's regiment was sent to a territory that had not yet decided whether it would be a free or slave state. Name it.

8. What famous abolitionist did he meet there?

9. In the winter of 1858–59, Stuart obtained a patent for what invention?

10. When the John Brown raid occurred, Stuart was ordered to deliver a set of secret orders to Arlington. To whom did he deliver them?

11. After Stuart quit the army in 1861, what notification did he receive from the army?

12. What was Stuart's first rank and command given to him by Virginia?

13. To whom did Stuart have to report, under his orders?

14. Within two months, Stuart received a different rank and command from Virginia. What was it?

15. Two months after that, he received a commission from the Confederate Army. For what rank?

16. During the war's opening days, while operating on Stonewall Jackson's flank, Stuart came upon a Union detachment while riding alone. What did he do?

17. To what regiment did those federals belong?

18. What "secret" did Jeb Stuart's beard hide?

19. Because of his "secret," what was Jeb Stuart's nickname at West Point?

20. In what battle was Stuart killed and where?

The leaders mentioned earlier had many brilliant and inept men working for them. For historians and war buffs, their lives are every bit as interesting as those of the major players.

Other Union Generals

1. Who was the "Rock of Chickamaugua"?

2. What did Maj. Gen. George Thomas have in common with Winfield Scott and Admiral David Farragut?

3. When the future Union general James B. McPherson was graduated from West Point in 1853, what was his class standing?

4. What future Confederate general graduated 44th in that class?

5. While stationed at Alcatraz in 1859, what future Union general did McPherson meet?

6. What regiment did Sheridan command at Corinth?

7. Among which generals in history did Grant rank Sheridan?

8. At West Point as a cadet, Sheridan nearly ended his military career early because of a severe breach of discipline. What did he do?

9. What was Sheridan's punishment?

10. With what Napoleonic relative did Sheridan serve in Texas, with the 1st Infantry, before the war?

11. To what office was Union general Ben Butler elected in 1882?

12. For what position was Butler considered by Lincoln, though Lincoln never followed through on his thought?

13. To what party did Butler belong to before the war?

14. At the 1860 Convention in Charleston, whom was Butler supposed to vote for?

15. Whom did Butler really vote for? How many times?

Other Confederate Generals

1. Confederate general Joseph E. Johnston married Polly Wood. What famous Revolutionary War politician was she related to?

2. During the Mexican War, what did Winfield Scott say of Johnston?

3. What Confederate army did Johnston command at the war's beginning?

4. How was Johnston wounded while defending Richmond?

5. Which Union general did Johnston surrender to at the war's end?

6. To what unit was Ambrose P. Hill assigned after he was graduated from West Point?

7. What Confederate regiment did A. P. Hill first command?

8. For his part in what battle was Hill promoted to lieutenant general?

9. At what battle was Hill killed?

10. To what unit was James Longstreet assigned after he was graduated from West Point?

11. When the war broke out and Longstreet resigned from the army, what position and rank did he have?

12. At the First Battle of Manassas, how big was the unit Longstreet commanded?

13. What was the nickname given to Longstreet by his troops?

14. Under what other Confederate Army general did Longstreet temporarily serve as a corps commander?

15. At what battle was Longstreet wounded?

The movement to abolish slavery was passionate and northern-based. It produced a best-selling book and an illegal movement helping runaway slaves.

Abolitionists

1. What book written before the war fueled abolitionist frenzy in the North? Who wrote it?

2. What famous church in present-day Brooklyn Heights was the place of many abolitionist rallies?

3. Who was the pastor of that church?

4. What political party organized in 1840 won the support of many black abolitionists?

5. What political party founded by disaffected Democrats in New York also received black abolitionist support in 1848?

6. In 1855, noted black abolitionists Frederick Douglass, J. W. Louguen and Amos G. Beman joined Gerrit Smith in which political party?

7. In early 1860, Douglass did not immediately support Abraham Lincoln. Why?

8. What noted nineteenth-century suffragette went on a speaking tour favoring emancipation?

9. In July 1864, how many petition signatures were already gathered favoring a constitutional amendment abolishing slavery?

10. What was the "Port Royal Experiment"?

Underground Railroad

1. What was the Underground Railroad?

2. Which routes between two states helped more slaves get away than any others?

3. Which Underground Railroad conductor was nicknamed "Moses"?

4. From what state did "Moses" escape?

5. What future Supreme Court Chief Justice was a lawyer in many fugitive slave cases?

6. When was it made a penal offense to help a runaway slave, and what was the law that made it so?

7. Who was the reputed president of the Underground Railroad?

8. What two principles not yet embodied in statutes were usually cited by Underground Railroad operators when they were prosecuted?

9. What Ohio college was a busy "station" on the Underground Railroad?

10. When was the last time the Ohio Legislature tried to repeal the charter of that college? What was the vote?

The United States had a government during the war which had its share of political differences and debate. This is sometimes overlooked because of the war's military element, which always tends to overshadow the politics.

Politics during the War—Union

1. What constitutional right did Lincoln suspend during the war?

2. Who made up Lincoln's first Cabinet?

3. After the Battle of Antietam, the political climate became right for the issuance of what order by Lincoln?

4. Whom did Lincoln appoint to succeed Chief Justice Roger Taney in 1864?

5. What post was given to Secretary of War Simon Cameron after he asked Lincoln to replace him?

6. Who replaced Cameron as Secretary of War?

7. The Emancipation Proclamation eliminated the interest of what country that wanted to recognize the Confederacy?

8. Who was nominated as Lincoln's running mate in 1864?

9. Who was the U.S. Ambassador to England during the Civil War?

10. Where were the worst draft riots of the war in the North?

11. What former Union general ran against Lincoln in 1864?

Politics during the War—Confederate

1. What was the first capital of the Confederacy?

2. When the decision was made to move the capital to Richmond, which state's delegation protested?

3. In 1861, the Arizona Territory declared it was part of the Confederacy. Whom did it send to Richmond to lobby for Arizona's admission as a Confederate Territory?

4. Who was the vice-president of the Confederate States of America?

5. Who made up Jefferson Davis's first Cabinet?

6. In November 1861, which states had provisions for absentee voting by its soldiers?

7. Under Confederate conscription law, how much did one have to pay to get a substitute to serve in one's place?

8. By 1864, how many regiments and battalions were going to be eligible for discharge once their three-year enlistments expired?

9. When introduced in 1864 in the Confederate Senate, how far did Senate Bill No. 158 extend the draft?

10. What percentage of Congress did Davis's opponents control between 1863 and the war's end?

The war began here, with the fledgling Confederate forces already in possession of other federal installations in Charleston harbor.

Fort Sumter

1. Who commanded Fort Sumter?

2. What four warships were to be dispatched to Fort Sumter in April 1861?

3. The *Powhatan* was the flagship of the force. Where was it dispatched instead?

4. Who commanded Confederate forces in Charleston?

5. What unit did Anderson command at Sumter?

6. How many men were stationed at Sumter?

7. At what time did the Confederates begin firing on Fort Sumter?

8. Who fired the first shot?

9. What regiment of South Carolina volunteers manned the fortification on Morris Island?

10. When was Anderson sure to run out of provisions?

11. What future Union general, who would later command a corps at Gettysburg temporarily, was at Sumter as a captain?

12. What ships were finally awaiting to reinforce Sumter on April 12?

13. Who fired the first Union shot? When? At which Confederate battery?

14. How many cartridges did Anderson have at the start of the siege?

15. Upon nightfall, what did Anderson order his men to do? Why?

16. On the second day of the siege, Anderson restricted fire toward one Confederate position. Which one?

17. How many barrels of gunpowder did Sumter store?

18. What ex-senator from Texas, who was not charged by Beauregard to represent him, got to run up the white flag for Anderson?

19. How many shots were put into Sumter in thirty-four hours of bombardment?

20. Nobody was killed in the shelling of Fort Sumter, but one person died while salutes were fired during Confederate ceremonies taking the fort over. Who was this person, the first casualty of the Civil War?

The war at sea was as strategically important as the war on land. The Civil War also saw several military innovations in the navies of both sides that spelled the end of wooden ships.

Naval War

1. What was the name of the first Confederate ironclad? From the remains of what Union ship was it built?

2. Where was the *Monitor* built?

3. Who was the famous American naval officer, world-

renowned for his work in charting currents and winds, who joined the Confederate Navy?

4. Who was the Confederate secretary of the navy? What was his senate committee assignment before the Civil War?

5. Who was the first commander of the *C.S.S. Virginia*?

6. Name the two Union warships sunk by the *Virginia*.

7. Who designed the *Monitor*?

8. Who was the first commander of the *Monitor*?

9. What kind of guns did the *Monitor* mount?

10. Who was the *Virginia*'s second commander?

11. Name the Confederate ironclad that defended Mobile Bay.

12. What was the Union flagship at the Battle of Mobile Bay, and who commanded the Union naval forces at that battle?

13. What were "ninety-day gunboats"?

14. What were torpedo boats?

15. What was a torpedo?

16. Who was the headstrong American naval commander who nearly brought the union to war with England over the Trent Affair?

17. While advancing on New Orleans, the Union ship

U.S.S. *Richmond* was rammed by which Confederate ironclad?

18. What were the names of the four Union ironclads used to take Fort Henry?

19. Who commanded Grant's river flotilla during the assault on Fort Henry?

20. What did the Union flotilla commander tell his gunners before they opened fire on Fort Henry?

21. What Union ironclad managed to run past the Confederate guns on Island No. 10?

22. What Confederate ironclad challenged the Union fleet bound for Vicksburg, and where was it built?

23. What was that ironclad's destination as it sailed down the Mississippi and riddled the Union fleet with shot?

24. What two Confederate ironclads were built to defend Charleston harbor?

25. What did those ironclads accomplish?

26. Who was the Union naval officer charged with the task of taking Charleston harbor on the second anniversary of the firing on Fort Sumter?

27. Name the Union ironclads used on that particular assault on Charleston.

28. What was the *Fingal* noted for?

29. What prevented the *Fingal* from going back to England?

30. What did the Confederates later do with the *Fingal*?

31. Name the two Union ironclads that engaged the *C.S.S. Atlanta*.

32. Where was the pilothouse located on second-model Monitors?

33. What were the *Monitor*'s two nicknames?

34. Name the admiral who was sent to relieve DuPont at Charleston, and name the admiral who shortly succeeded that replacement.

35. The Confederate torpedo boat *David* tried to sink which Union ironclad at Charleston?

36. Name the first submarine, which side it fought for, and which ship it sank. (That ship was the first ever to be sunk by a sub.)

37. Name the Confederate ironclad built to defend Albermarle Sound.

38. What coastal city did that ironclad help retake?

39. Which Union warships did it defeat in battle?

40. Who was the Union commander who sank the *Albermarle*?

41. How did he do it?

42. What was the name of the first commerce cutter built for the Confederacy in England, and what was it later renamed?

43. Where and how was the *C.S.S. Florida* finally captured, and what international law was violated?

44. What was the second commerce cruiser built for the Confederacy in England, and what was it later renamed?

45. Who commanded the *C.S.S. Alabama*?

46. Who commanded the *C.S.S. Florida*?

47. While masquerading as a British warship, the *Alabama* surprised and sank a Union warship outside of Galveston. Name the union warship.

48. When the *Alabama* put into Cherbourg, the *U.S.S. Kearsage* was notified of her presence by the American consul there. Where was the *Kearsage* when it got word?

49. Who commanded the *Kearsage*?

50. When the *Kearsage* and the *Alabama* fought it out outside of Cherbourg, who won?

51. Name the only Confederate warship to have circumnavigated the world.

Campaigns were the great moves behind the big battles. In some cases, the strategic thinking behind some campaigns was sound, if not brilliant, but putting that thinking into action left something to be desired.

McClellan's Peninsular Campaign sounded good on paper because it advocated taking Richmond by indirect means, namely an amphibious landing south of it. Sherman's March to the Sea underscored the importance of destroying the economic means of making war as well as the armies in the field. Stonewall Jackson's campaign in the Shenandoah Valley is a classic study of hit and run, as his inferior force held off several Union armies.

Shenandoah Valley, 1862

1. By mid-March, how many men were in Jackson's "Valley Army"?

2. Which Union general's detachment did Jackson attack first in late March? Where was the battle?

3. What were the numbers for each side? Who won?

4. Whose total command of Union troops was stripped to

provide Banks an autonomous department to chase after Jackson?

5. Who was given command of the Union Mountain Department, which flanked the Shenandoah Valley?

6. Whose corps was not sent to reinforce McClellan on the Peninsula so that a force could be kept between the Shenandoah Valley and Washington?

7. What was the number of the huge B. & O. locomotive Jackson had dragged cross-country to Staunton in an effort to reclaim rolling stock?

8. By the end of April, how many men were in Jackson's Army?

9. What Union general did Jackson attack at McDowell? To whose Union army did he belong?

10. What was the nickname given to Jackson's infantry which covered a great deal of ground in the Shenandoah Campaign in a short time?

11. What Southern military school furnished a unit which was later withdrawn so that they could resume their studies?

12. At the end of April, whose Confederate division entered the Valley to support Jackson?

13. What Confederate regiment commander under Jackson had challenged him to a duel back in Virginia Military Institute? What regiment did he command?

14. What Louisiana regimental commander later gained

fame after the war as a soldier of fortune in Cuba, Nicaragua, Mexico, and Italy with Garibaldi?

15. On May 23, where did Jackson defeat a small Union garrison?

16. Marching North to Winchester, whose army did Jackson attack on May 25?

17. By June, Frémont was closing in on Jackson from the mountains to the west and Shields was marching from the east from McDowell's Corps to attack Jackson as well. Where did Jackson attack Frémont?

18. Where did Jackson stop Shields?

19. How many days separated the two battles?

20. How many Union soldiers did Jackson tie up in their pursuit of his tiny army?

Peninsular Campaign—Spring, 1862

1. What Virginia city on what river did McClellan originally plan to take on his advance toward Richmond?

2. Where did McClellan land the Army of the Potomac instead?

3. McClellan planned to outflank the Confederate line stretching from Yorktown parallel with the Warwick

River, but the unit that would actually do this was kept in Washington. Whose unit was it?

4. How many guns did McClellan capture when the Confederates gave up their line?

5. What river forced McClellan to split his army in two, thus leaving one position operating north of it and another south of it?

6. What untried military instrument did McClellan use to check Confederate defenses on the Warwick River and who brought this "instrument" with him?

7. What battle resulted when the Confederates tried to defeat the Union troops south of the river?

8. Who commanded Confederate forces until he was wounded at Fair Oaks?

9. Whom did Jefferson Davis replace him with?

10. Which Union corps was the target of a three-pronged attack at Fair Oaks?

11. What two Confederate generals kept the Union Army occupied north of the river during the battle?

12. What Confederate general took 1200 cavalry troops for a three-day ride around McClellan's army to gather information?

13. What is the name given to the series of battles outside of Richmond after the immortal three-day ride?

14. During what battle did Stonewall Jackson's Valley Army fail to support an attack by A. P. Hill?

15. Porter's Corps, which had to retreat during this battle, was hit again the next day (June 27) and was again forced to retreat south of the river. Name the battle.

16. Union losses here forced McClellan to transfer his base of operations from what river to what river?

17. Lee tried to outflank McClellan's supply line to Harrison's landing. What battle resulted from the attempt by A. P. Hill and Longstreet to do so?

18. On July 1, the Confederates tried to take a strong Union holding north of Harrison's Landing. What was this battle?

19. Whose two Confederate units attacked up the hill and suffered great losses?

20. How many reinforcements was Lincoln willing to send McClellan at this campaign's end? What did McClellan say to this proposition?

Red River Campaign

1. One objective of this campaign was the invasion of which state?

2. What product vital to the South's economy was also the target of this campaign?

3. What general led the campaign?

4. What was the name of Admiral Porter's flagship in this campaign?

5. What was the name of the Confederate fort at Yellow Bayou which was abandoned in the face of the Union advance?

6. Where did Union forces capture most of Confederate General Taylor's cavalry in a railroad camp?

7. What natural event that failed to take place prevented Admiral Porter from bringing his ironclads beyond Alexandria, Louisiana?

8. Despite this, the heaviest ironclad in the fleet was chosen to make passage into the Upper Red River. What ship was that?

9. Who commanded a regiment of German cavalry troops from Texas for the Confederacy?

10. At what battle was a portion of the Union Army repulsed by the Confederate general Richard Taylor?

Sherman's Advance toward Atlanta and the Subsequent Battles for Atlanta

1. What Confederate general did Sherman face? Name the Confederate corps commanders.

2. Name the three armies Sherman commanded and name who led them.

3. Where was the first defensive position Johnston took facing Sherman?

4. Which Union army advanced beyond Johnston's left to Resaca, thus threatening Johnston's supply line?

5. How many men stopped McPherson at Resaca?

6. What strong Confederate unit joined Johnston at Resaca and who commanded it?

7. What compelled Johnston to withdraw from Resaca after fighting a three-day battle there?

8. After six weeks of pursuing Johnston and slipping around his flank, Sherman made a futile frontal assault on June 27. Name the battle.

9. At what point on the Chattahoochee River did Sherman force a crossing?

10. When was Johnston relieved of his command of the Army of Tennessee?

11. Who replaced Johnston?

12. How many men were in the Army of Tennessee when Johnston's replacement took command? How many Union soldiers did he face?

13. Where did Hood attack Thomas's Army? How many men did he lose?

14. Which corps did Hood send around to the southeast to attack the Union flank on July 22?

15. What Union general was killed in this attack?

16. Who was given command of this dead general's army?

17. Where was the next battle for Atlanta, when, and whose units participated?

18. What cavalry commander's force was sent on a raid by Hood to tear up the railroad between Chattanooga and Atlanta?

19. Where and when was the last battle for Atlanta?

20. When did Hood evacuate Atlanta?

Sherman's March to the Sea

1. Which Confederate general did Sherman give up pursuing shortly before his "March to the Sea"?

2. How many wings did Sherman reorganize his army into?

3. Who commanded the wings?

4. When did Sherman's army leave Atlanta?

5. With no supply line backing his army, what did Sherman have his troops do?

6. How much damage did Sherman's March to the Sea inflict, in terms of dollars?

7. How much of the damage was "useful to the army" and how much of it was waste, according to Sherman?

8. Upon capturing Savannah, what Confederate general and his army did Sherman let get away? How many men did he have?

9. What fort did Sherman's Army have to storm to take Savannah?

10. The notable "battle" in the March was a skirmish between Sherman's troops and the Georgia Militia. Where was it?

Hood's Winter Offensive

1. What was the strategic objective of Hood's winter offensive of 1864?

2. How many men did Hood have?

3. Which general did Sherman leave in Atlanta while he pursued Hood?

4. How many days did Hood's army spend ripping up rails and telegraph lines at Allatoona?

5. What small town did Hood demand a surrender from or face the threat of being taken by storm? What happened?

6. After tiring of the pursuit of Hood, what did Sherman do?

7. What Union general's force did Hood bypass to go north of? Where was it?

8. Hood blocked Schofield's path of retreat at Spring Hill. What happened next?

9. What did Schofield plan to do after he left Franklin on November 30?

10. What did Hood do when he came upon Franklin?

11. How many men charged the Federal breastworks at Franklin?

12. How many were killed?

13. How many generals did Hood lose in the bloody charge and how many of those were killed?

14. How many men did Hood have when he reached Nashville?

15. Whom did Sherman send to defend Tennessee against Hood?

16. How many men did this general have?

17. How long was Hood encamped above Nashville before the attack?

18. This general's fierce attack penetrated Hood's left flank and forced him back a few miles. What happened next?

19. How many men did Hood have after suffering these attacks?

20. Where did the shattered army finally retreat?

Final Campaigns

1. At what plantation landing did Union forces try to slip in two corps to take Petersburg?

2. Who commanded this force?

3. After finding out Petersburg could not be taken from the north, what major city north of the plantation landing did this commander want to take?

4. At what Confederate position was this commander driven back?

5. Who commanded the Confederate troops there?

6. At what point did Lee defend the North Anna River crossing after Grant tried to slip around his right flank after Spotsylvania?

7. Where did Grant cross his army on the Pamunkey River?

8. On May 29, Lee sent two cavalry brigades to make a reconnaissance of the Union positions. Where was the major cavalry clash?

9. What crossroads did Lee try to have seized by cavalry and also became the site of a cavalry engagement?

10. How many men charged the entrenched Confederate army at Cold Harbor?

11. How long did the charge last?

12. How many Union soldiers died?

13. In an effort to move around Lee's army, whose corps did Grant send to Bermuda Hundred to take Petersburg?

14. What Confederate position did the commander of this corps assault and capture a portion of?

15. What Confederate unit contained Butler at Bermuda Hundred, after Bushrod Johnson's unit was sent to Petersburg?

16. How many men did Beauregard have to face Grant's 75,000 men at Petersburg?

17. Whose corps helped bolster the Confederates at Petersburg?

18. Which two Union corps tried to cut the Weldon Railroad to Petersburg?

19. A. P. Hill drove both corps in separate attacks back across what road?

20. In July of 1864, what engineering feat was resorted to in an effort to blow up a section of Confederate line at Petersburg?

The war had its share of daring exploits, where small bands of men wreaked havoc behind Union lines and disappeared before the Union knew what hit them. One such Confederate guerrilla, William Quantrill, had several men under his command that would later achieve greater fame after the war as outlaws.

Early's Raid

1. Whose 5,000-man army did Early try to capture at Harpers Ferry?

2. From Sharpsburg, Maryland, Early sent a cavalry brigade to Hagerstown to extort money for damage caused to the Shenandoah Valley by Union forces. How much did Early want? How much was brought back?

3. What town in Maryland did Early occupy to get the rest of the money he required from the local populace?

4. Whose corps did Grant detach to keep Early out of Washington?

5. How many Union troops were there between Early's position and Washington when they arrived?

6. Who commanded this improvised Union force?

7. With these five thousand reinforcements, where did he try to hold Early, only to be driven back?

8. What fort that was part of Washington's defensive ring did Early occupy?

9. The Union corps marched up which road to stage a night attack to retake this fort?

10. Early crossed which Potomac River ford to get back into Virginia?

Quantrill's Raids

1. On whose Western expedition did Quantrill serve before the war?

2. Who was Quantrill's right-hand man in his Missouri guerrilla band?

3. March 30, 1861. What happened to Quantrill's gang at the Clark Farm?

4. In late July 1862, a Union detachment ambushed three of Quantrill's men. Which two died? Which one escaped harm?

5. What did General Order Number 19 call for in Missouri?

6. Confederate Col. John T. Hughes teamed up with Quantrill to take which Missouri town at the war's beginning?

7. In what small Missouri battle did Quantrill raider Cole Younger first gain fame?

8. What Kansas town that was a hotbed of abolitionism became the target of a massacre by Quantrill's band?

9. What was General Ewing's Order Number 11?

10. What incident forced Quantrill from command of his band?

Morgan's Raids

1. What was the name of Morgan's horse?

2. Out of what Kentucky town were Morgan and his men forced by a strong Union column after Shiloh?

3. How much Union money did Morgan's men make off with after the raid on Cave City?

4. What regiment did Morgan raise after the Cave City raid of 1862?

5. On his second Kentucky raid, what was Morgan's first objective?

Nathan Bedford Forrest's Raids

1. At what major battle early in the war was Forrest wounded?

2. What Union general did Forrest capture at Murfreesboro?

3. With the death of Van Dorn, what command did Forrest assume?

4. How many men did Forrest have when he defeated Grierson's 7,000 men at the plains of Okolona?

5. What Union raider did he capture after a forty-eight-hour pursuit in Rome, Georgia?

The battles are the milestones of the war. Often bloody, they involved tens of thousands of men using weapons whose killing capabilities were well beyond the outdated tactics used by their generals. Gettysburg stands out as the dramatic climax of the war. Vicksburg, however, overshadowed that battle because of its strategic importance, and was the real turning point of the war. Shiloh and Antietam were the earliest of the bloody battles that erased the holiday atmosphere of the war. Chancellorsville stands as the best example of how a gamble can pay off when an opportunity is seen and taken, while Chickamauga and Fredericksburg are tragic because of the opportunities that were seen and lost.

First Manassas

1. Who commanded the Union Army at the First Battle of Manassas?

2. What was Bull Run?

3. Where did McDowell make his headquarters before moving into Virginia?

4. What was the objective of McDowell's first campaign?

5. Why was McDowell in a hurry to fight the battle?

6. What Union general was stationed with 14,000 troops in Maryland? What was his purpose?

7. What previous wars did that Union general fight in?

8. What rank did Stonewall Jackson have in the battle?

9. Where was the first skirmish of the battle fought?

10. What was McDowell's plan at Bull Run?

11. Where was McDowell supposed to strike his northern blow?

12. Who were the two Union divisional commanders that made this northern attack?

13. The first civilian casualty of the Civil War died in this battle. Who was it and where?

14. Name the three Confederate commanders whose units held out at Matthews Hill.

15. Where did Jackson deploy his brigade?

16. Whose Union unit made a demonstration at the Confederate center?

17. What Union brigadier at Bull Run, supported by Tyler's unit, managed to force back part of the Confederate line?

18. What Confederate general had a horse shot out from under him at the battle?

19. How many senators and congressmen came out from Washington to have a picnic and watch the battle?

20. Which Confederate regiment captured a Union battery because they wore blue uniforms?

Shiloh

1. What distinguished Shiloh from the battles fought before it?

2. Who commanded the Confederate Army at Shiloh?

3. U. S. Grant commanded one of the Union armies at Shiloh. How old was he at that time?

4. Grant and his Confederate counterpart had one political problem in common before Shiloh. What was it?

5. What important rail crossing might Grant have captured before Shiloh had he been given a free hand by Halleck?

6. What was the name of Grant's army at Shiloh? What was the name of Johnston's army?

7. What famous future Union commander commanded the Fifth Division?

8. What famous future Confederate commander was in charge of Johnston's Second Corps?

9. What recent vice-president of the United States commanded a Confederate corps at Shiloh?

10. Name the first Union and Confederate units to trade shots at Shiloh.

11. What was the name of the mongrel mascot of the 6th Iowa Regiment at Shiloh?

12. On the first day of the battle, the Confederate Army was blessed with one advantage that, for them, would be rare in the war. What was it?

13. What were Johnston's famous words on the first day of the battle?

14. What Confederate regiment was fired upon by their own comrades and why?

15. What medical "first" occurred at Shiloh?

16. This area, held by Union commanders Hurlburt on the left and W. H. L. Wallace on the right, was the scene of some of the bloodiest fighting in the battle. What was this position nicknamed by the Confederates?

17. What tactic did Bragg use in trying to take this position?

18. Where did Johnston suffer his fatal wound?

19. What Union division suffered the highest casualties from the battle?

20. What Union army joined Grant in the battle and who commanded it?

Second Manassas

1. Who commanded the Union forces at the Second Battle of Manassas?

2. What was the army he commanded named?

3. Where was the Army of the Potomac at this time?

4. At the opening of the battle, what Union general led the attack, and whose corps did he assault?

5. What Union general was later court-martialed because of his failure in the battle to move his units?

6. Which Confederate commander's corps hit Pope's flank, forcing him to retreat?

7. From what campaign did Porter's corps come?

8. What geographic entity did Jackson exploit to give his line greater strength?

9. Where did Longstreet's attack drive the Federals?

10. What were the casualties for both sides?

Antietam

1. Prior to this battle, Jackson captured an important river junction on September 15. What was it? How many Union troops did he capture?

2. What was the name of the nearby town at the Battle of Antietam?

3. How badly was Lee outnumbered at Antietam?

4. In terms of casualties, what was Antietam noted for?

5. What was McClellan's battle plan at Antietam?

6. Who commanded the Union forces at the northern end of the battlefield?

7. The farthest limit of Hooker's advance against the Confederates was to what landmark?

8. What two Confederate generals finally stopped Hooker's attack?

9. What wound did Hooker suffer?

10. What was the nickname of the sunken road the Confederates defended at the center of their line?

11. What Union general was in charge of forces at the southern end of the battlefield?

12. Across what body of water did Burnside attack?

13. What landmark on the battlefield was later named after Burnside?

14. Who held the Confederate position overlooking the bridge? What kind of forces did he have?

15. What battlefield landmark did Hooker advance across?

16. When Burnside was taking the bluffs above Antietam Creek, whose division arrived in the nick of time to save the Confederates?

17. Where did that unit march from? How far away was that place?

18. How many men did McClellan lose in the battle?

19. How many men did Lee lose in the battle?

20. What political move resulted from the Union's holding its own in the battle?

Fredericksburg

1. Who commanded the Union army at Fredericksburg? Who commanded the Confederate army at Fredericksburg?

2. How many Confederates were in Fredericksburg when Burnside showed up with a 120,000-man army on November 17, 1862?

3. Where was Lee's army at this time?

4. For what did Burnside have to wait until November 22?

5. Whose fault was the delay?

6. What was the weather like on the morning the Union army stormed the Confederate lines?

7. What Confederate general held the line at Hamilton's Crossing?

8. Which Confederate general held the positions at Marye's Heights?

9. What was the closest the Union troops got to the stone wall at Marye's Heights?

10. Who commanded the Union's central Grand Division?

11. What did Hooker do when he received orders to storm Marye's Heights?

12. Who commanded the Union assault at Hamilton's Crossing?

13. How many men did Franklin dispatch to attack Jackson's 35,000 men?

14. Who commanded this unit that attacked Jackson?

15. What did he encounter in the attack?

16. What was the result of the attack?

17. How many men did the Union lose? How many men did the Confederates lose?

18. What officer of Stuart's cavalry harassed Franklin's advance?

19. How many guns did he have?

20. From which state did the soldiers in Meade's division come?

Murfreesboro

1. What was the other name for this battle?

2. Who replaced Don Carlos Buell to command the Union army that fought here?

3. Where was the army based?

4. What was the nickname given to Rosecrans by his troops?

5. When the Confederate corps under Hardee attacked the Union corps under McCook, whose Union division held its ground?

6. What geographic position on the battlefield did the Union hold against Polk's attack?

7. What Confederate general was killed in the attack on the Round Forest?

8. What was another name for the Round Forest?

9. Whose Federal brigade held the Round Forest?

10. What happened on New Year's Day at this battle?

11. On January 2, what move did Rosecrans make?

12. From whose corps did the division come?

13. When ordered by Bragg to take the hill across the river on the Union left, how did Breckinridge react?

14. Who won the battle for the hill?

15. What forced the Confederates to give up the hill?

16. What were the approximate losses to both armies?

17. How much of the Union army was AWOL or in the hospital when Rosecrans took command before the battle?

18. What pressure did Rosecrans face from Washington when he took command?

19. What did Rosecrans call his staff officers?

20. Rosecrans got authority to do what to errant officers while the army was on the move?

Chancellorsville

1. Who commanded the Union army at Chancellorsville?

2. What was the Union's grand strategy at Chancellorsville?

3. Who commanded the Union forces at Fredericksburg while Hooker was at Chancellorsville?

4. What Confederate unit withdrew before the battle in the face of a strong Union advance?

5. Union Cavalry commander Alfred Pleasonton scored a small coup that would have an effect on the battle when it came later. What was the nature of the coup?

6. What kind of information resulted from the coup?

7. What was the "meeting in the woods."

8. What news were Lee and Jackson waiting for about the Union right flank?

9. Fitzhugh Lee, who served under Jeb Stuart, uncovered an important piece of information about the Union dispositions. What was it?

10. Whom did Lee leave at Marye's Heights to make sure the army at Fredericksburg stayed put?

11. What was Hooker's nickname?

12. What was the risk Lee took at Chancellorsville?

13. What time of day did Jackson begin his great flanking march?

14. How many men did Jackson have?

15. How many men was Lee left with?

16. How big was the Union army that they faced?

17. Which one of Hooker's corps commanders was not a graduate of West Point?

18. What was the name of the region Jackson marched through that would later be the site of another famous battle?

19. What did Sickles find out when his troops captured several Confederates? What did Sickles believe?

20. Who commanded the Union's XI Corps, and what was a noticeable physical characteristic about him?

21. How was the XI Corps looked upon by the Army of the Potomac, and why?

22. At 5:15 A.M. on May 2, what happened to the XI Corps?

23. What divisional commander in Jackson's corps would later himself become a corps commander?

24. How did Jackson die in this battle?

25. Who took command of Jackson's corps temporarily following Jackson's death?

Vicksburg

1. What value did Lincoln place on Vicksburg?

2. Why is Vicksburg important?

3. Who commanded the Confederate army of Mississippi at Vicksburg? What was notable about him?

4. What powerful Illinois Democrat was empowered by Lincoln to raise an army to take Vicksburg?

5. How was McClernand's army supposed to be handled shortly after it was raised?

6. What was McClernand's first operation?

7. What fruitless battle did Sherman fight north of Vicksburg? What were the casualties?

8. When Grant took command of the 60,000-man Union army at Vicksburg, he divided it into three corps. Who were the corps commanders?

9. From what direction did Grant think Vicksburg could be taken?

10. Where was Grant's HQ at the start of the Vicksburg campaign?

11. Grant was committed to a river strategy in his campaign. What engineering feat did he resort to in order to bypass Vicksburg?

12. Was this venture a success? Why?

13. How long were the immediate Confederate lines defending Vicksburg?

14. What Confederate position on the Tallahatchie River repulsed a Union gunboat flotilla looking for a water route north of Vicksburg?

15. Grant marched his army to what point on the west bank of the Mississippi River south of Vicksburg to meet his flotilla?

16. What did the flotilla have to do to meet Grant's army?

17. Unaware of Grant's strategy, Pemberton detached part of his army and sent it to the aid of another Confederate general. Who was that general, and how many men was Pemberton going to send to him?

18. When those troops were sent, how many were there?

19. What point on the east bank of the Mississippi did Grant's men have to capture before crossing?

20. What Confederate-held landing had to be captured to open a supply line southward to New Orleans?

21. Without a supply line, Grant crossed his army and landed on the east bank of the Mississippi at what point?

22. Grant sent out a cavalry column that rode all the way from Grand Junction to Baton Rouge. Who led it? What was his prewar profession?

23. What state capital did Grant capture east of Vicksburg?

24. When Grant relieved McClernand, whom did he appoint to replace him?

25. What did Grant do with the captured Confederates after Vicksburg fell on July 3, 1863?

Gettysburg

1. Which Union corps commander was killed on the first day of the battle?

2. Who took over command of the Union I Corps after that general was killed?

3. What three corps were under the command of that general who was killed on the first day?

4. Who commanded the Union's Army of the Potomac at Gettysburg?

5. Name Lee's corps commanders.

6. Whose divisions from each army made initial contact on the first day of battle?

7. What was important about Little Round Top?

8. What was Lee's move on the second day?

9. What was Longstreet's suggestion?

10. Why was Lee reluctant to take Longstreet's suggestion?

11. What corps was the anchor of the Union's right flank and where?

12. What Union regiment held the far left of the line at Little Round Top?

13. Whose corps was the first to engage the Union army?

14. What was the name of the rock outcropping that the Confederates took opposite of Little Round Top?

15. What were the names of two areas northwest of the rock outcropping that were both scenes of bloody fighting?

16. What was Lee's objective on the third day of the battle?

17. Whose division was to spearhead the attack?

18. Name the ridge the Confederates occupied opposite the Union position on Cemetery Ridge?

19. What other divisions were designated to accompany Pickett?

20. What distinguished Pickett's division from other units at the Battle of Gettysburg?

21. From what state were the men in Pickett's division?

22. What Union regiments fired on Pickett's right flank at the charge's climax?

23. What other Union regiment did the same to Pickett on his left flank?

24. In one of the greatest ironies of the battle, a Confederate general in Pickett's division was leading his brigade against the corps of a Union general who was his best friend before the war. Name them both.

25. After "Pickett's Charge," how many men answered roll call the next day? (Not all of them were fit for duty.) How many men were in his division before the charge?

Chickamauga

1. What corps from the Army of Northern Virginia was sent to Bragg before the battle?

2. What was numerically unusual about this battle?

3. What religious distinction belonged to one of Bragg's corps commanders, Leonidas Polk?

4. What did Bragg hope to do to Rosecrans' army before Chickmauga?

5. What two units first made contact at Chickamauga and where?

6. What was Bragg's immediate objective in the battle and why was it important?

7. The arrival of whose corps helped the Union hold Lafayette Road on the first day?

8. On the second day of the battle, Bragg divided his command in two. Who commanded each wing?

9. On the second day of the battle, what was the Confederate plan?

10. The delay in Polk's attack allowed Rosecrans to do what?

11. Units belonging to which Confederate general managed to break through Rosecrans' line?

12. After Thomas dispersed two Confederate brigades to his rear, he asked Rosecrans for reinforcements. Whose division did Rosecrans send?

13. That troop movement caused what to happen to the Union right? What happened?

14. What happened to the Union line when Longstreet attacked?

15. What did Rosecrans do when his line collapsed?

16. What position did Thomas take?

17. Whose reserve corps helped fortify Thomas' line?

18. What did Thomas do at nightfall after holding the Confederates off?

19. What did Longstreet want to do after the battle? What was Bragg's reaction?

20. What were the approximate losses for both sides?

Chattanooga

1. What was the name of the prominent mountain over-looking Moccasin Point?

2. What was the name of the ridge held by the Confederates overlooking Chattanooga?

3. What Union general was sent to Chattanooga with a corps from the Army of the Potomac?

4. When Grant was given command of all forces, whom did he replace Rosecrans with?

5. Because the Confederates held Lookout Mountain, what condition was the Union army in Chattanooga left in?

6. Whose corps did Grant use to reestablish the supply line, and what was that position called?

7. What ferry north of Chattanooga did the Union take, and who commanded the force that did this?

8. Which union general was ordered to cross the ferry and attack the Confederate line on northern Missionary Ridge?

9. Which Confederate general was in command of forces on Lookout Mountain?

10. What Confederate general and his corps was sent from Chattanooga to Knoxville?

11. What was the name of the hill Sherman attacked?

12. Which general commanded the corps at this sector? Whom did he replace?

13. Who was the Irish-born Confederate general whose division held the hill that Sherman attacked?

14. What piece of terrain did Grant order Thomas to take that was halfway between the Union and Confederate lines?

15. When Grant ordered Thomas to advance up Missionary Ridge, how far up were Thomas' men supposed to go?

16. Was Sherman ever successful in taking the hill he attacked?

17. How many divisions did Thomas have?

18. What happened after Thomas' men reached the base of Missionary Ridge?

19. To what Georgia rail town did Bragg's army withdraw?

20. Which Confederate division fought as a rear guard during this retreat?

Battle of the Wilderness and Spotsylvania

1. Who were the Union corps commanders at this battle?

2. How good was the visibility in this battle?

3. When a brigade of Texans formerly commanded by Hood appeared at the battlefield, what did Lee try to do with them?

4. What did the Texan brigade do?

5. Confederate general Gordon's division struck whose Union corps in the flank?

6. When the battle ended on May 7, what did Grant do with his army?

7. Whose army got to Spotsylvania first, Lee's or Grant's?

8. What Union corps commander was killed in the fighting?

9. What cavalry skirmish confirmed Lee's suspicion that Grant was moving on Spotsylvania?

10. Who took command of A. P. Hill's corps when Hill became ill?

11. On May 12, Grant sent sixty thousand men against a

salient in the Confederate line. What was this salient called?

12. Whose corps made the attack?

13. Whose Confederate division stopped the advance?

14. Was Gordon successful in retaking "The Mule Shoe"?

15. What was the Mule Shoe dubbed after this part of the battle?

16. Where was the first contact made in the Battle of the Wilderness between the two armies?

17. What famous Confederate general was wounded in the same woods where Stonewall Jackson was shot the year before?

18. Throughout the Wilderness and Spotsylvania, how long did Grant's army maintain contact with Lee's army?

19. How many men did each army lose?

20. To whom was these losses a greater setback?

The war had to end someplace. For the Army of Northern Virginia, it was at Appomattox where continuing the war against superior Union forces became pointless. The war did not end with Lee's surrender, but there was no way it could go on for long once he did.

Appomattox

1. What Union general's cavalry faced Lee at Appomattox?

2. Which cavalry general did Sheridan send to cut out the Confederate freight train at Appomattox station?

3. What song was played by a Northern band as Grant rode up to Appomattox Court House for Lee's surrender?

4. How many effectives could Lee's army muster on the last day of the war?

5. How many pieces of artillery did he have left?

6. How many cavalry did he have left?

7. What did Grant and Lee discuss before getting on with the business of surrender?

8. What were the conditions of surrender Grant gave Lee?

9. What weapons did not have to be surrendered?

10. What else would not be surrendered?

11. To what other Union general did Lee speak at Appomattox and why?

12. How many rations did Grant send to Lee's army?

13. On April 10, Lee was visited by five Union generals. Name them.

14. What souvenir did Sheridan get from the surrender and how much did he pay for it?

15. What did Sheridan do with his souvenir?

16. Which one of Lee's generals proposed an alternative to surrender and what was it?

17. Name the Union officer who brought Lee the letter from Grant suggesting surrender?

18. What did Fitzhugh Lee do about this time and why?

19. Lee thought Grant's terms of surrender would be harsh. What did Longstreet think?

20. Which corps of the Army of Northern Virginia staged the last attack of that army at war's end?

The Geneva Convention, which enumerates the rights of prisoners of war, was not yet adopted. Soldiers who were captured in battle sometimes suffered horribly in unhealthful camps like Andersonville.

Andersonville

1. Where was Andersonville?

2. How many acres was the site of the prisoner compound?

3. How many soldiers were crammed into it?

4. What was the "dead line"?

5. How many sentries guarded the prison?

6. How many cannons overlooked the prison and what kind were they?

7. What was the standard prisoner's ration at Andersonville?

8. What was the stream running through the camp used for?

9. How large was the swamp within the compound?

10. On the average, how many prisoners died daily?

The final tragedy of the war was Lincoln's assassination. After Lincoln had labored so long to attain a victory, a single bullet denied him the chance of seeing the fruits of his ordeal. Lincoln was the first American president to be assassinated. It was quite a shock in those days, compared to now, when such political violence is commonplace.

Lincoln's Assassination

1. Where was Lincoln when he was fatally shot?

2. What play was he seeing?

3. Who were the other two men targeted for assassination?

4. Who shot Lincoln? What weapon did he use?

5. President and Mrs. Lincoln were seeing the play with another couple. Who were they?

6. What happened to the male guest after Lincoln was shot?

7. What two phrases did the assassin utter after he shot the president?

8. What was the last line of dialogue in the play before the assassin pulled the trigger?

9. What happened to the assassin when he jumped to the stage from the president's theater box?

10. Which conspirator had the task of killing the secretary of state?

11. Who accompanied this conspirator to watch the horses?

12. Where was the intended victim when his attacker tried to kill him?

13. Did the victim survive the attack?

14. Who was supposed to kill the vice-president?

15. Did that conspirator go through with his mission?

16. Lincoln was taken across the street to a house where he later died. What was the name of the family that owned the house?

17. What cabinet official took effective control of the government while Lincoln was dying?

18. Whom did that cabinet official think was behind the assassination? What was he expecting?

19. Who was the physician who unknowingly set the assassin's leg?

20. What happened to the assassin? What happened to the other conspirators?

The North had to integrate the South politically back into the Union once the war was ended. But this was done under the arrogant heel of military occupation, and not all southerners took to it kindly.

Reconstruction

1. Who were the "Redeemers"?

2. What four Confederate states did not have their state governments abolished by President Andrew Johnson after the war ended?

3. What Confederates did Johnson's amnesty exclude?

4. What was the National Union Convention? When and where was it? What was its purpose?

5. What was the convention nicknamed and why?

6. In the elections of 1866, the Republicans controlled all the Northern states. Which three border states did they control as well?

7. Which three states did the Democrats control?

8. How many seats did the Republicans and the Democrats control in the House of Representatives after the 1866 election?

9. In December of 1866, the United States Supreme Court ruled that the president had no power to authorize trials of civilians by military courts in areas where civil courts were open. What was the case in question?

10. What restriction was brought on Southern states by the Command of the Army Act?

11. What was Grant's General Order Number 44?

12. Who was made the interim secretary of war when Johnson got Secretary of War Edward Stanton to resign?

13. What general did Johnson remove from command of the Third District? Who was Johnson's first choice for replacement?

14. Who actually accepted the position?

15. What did the First Reconstruction Act demand of the Southern states?

16. Who was the First Grand Wizard of the Ku Klux Klan? Who originally declined command of the K.K.K.?

17. What was the Klan designation for each state? What was the title of the state chairman?

18. What was the name of the entire area under Klan domination?

19. Where was the first Grand Wizard sworn in?

20. Who was the first Southern governor to be impeached by Klan effort, where and in what year?

Every war has its famous leaders uttering famous words. Which ones do you remember?

Quotations

Who said the following?

1. "The slightest straw almost would have kept the tide in our favor."

2. "It is well that war is so terrible; men would love it too much."

3. "War is Hell."

4. "Damn the torpedoes."

5. "That this nation under God, shall have a new birth of Freedom and that government of the people, by the people, for the people, shall not perish from the Earth."

6. "With malice toward none; with charity for all; with

firmness in the right, let us strive to finish the work we are in; to bind up the nation's wounds.''

7. "The Father of Waters again goes unvexed to the sea."

8. "It is the duty of every citizen, in the present condition of the country, to do all in his power to aid in the restoration of peace and harmony, and in no way oppose the policy of the state or General Government directed to that object."

9. "Order A. P. Hill to prepare for action! Pass the infantry to the front! No, no, let us pass over the river and rest under the shade of the trees."

10. "Yes, madam, it's very sad—very sad, and this thing has been going on in Virginia for more than two years—very sad."

11. "I am going fast now. I am resigned, God's will be done."

12. "Be of good cheer, for within a short while your faces will be turned homeward, and your feet pressing Tennessee soil."

13. "Within a few days, I expect to give the command 'Forward,' and I believe you are, like myself, willing to go forward, even if we live on parched corn and beef."

14. "If the thing is pressed, I think Lee will surrender."

15. "I need not tell the brave survivors, of so many hard-fought battles, who have remained steadfast to

the last, that I have consented to the result from no distrust of them.''

16. ''And after the battle, then the slain and wounded will arise, and all will meet together under the two flags, all sound and well, and there will be talking and laughter and cheer, and all will say: Did it seem real? Was it not as in the old days?''

17. ''I feel powerless to do good for my country, and humiliated by the acts of the people I was striving to benefit.''

18. ''I fancy, Sam, that we will never reach that land where it is all afternoon in any ship built by mortal hands.''

19. ''They treat me at Washington and at Grant's head-quarters as though I were a boy.''

20. ''The Army of the Potomac is in splendid condition and evidently feels like whipping somebody. I feel much better with this command than I did before seeing it.''

Some who were obscure during the war later gained fame in other endeavors. Some who were famous during the war went on to become distinguished and involved in other ventures. Still others left their names in the history book for simply being at the place where great events occurred.

Famous People during the War

1. This famous actor had a brother who later gained notoriety in a theater. Who was he?

2. This brevet cavalry general later died with his regiment in Montana when he was surrounded by Indians. Who was he?

3. This man, who ran a photo studio in New York, compiled a photographic record of the war, though many taken by his assistants were credited to him. Who was he?

4. This Union general is sometimes credited with creating an American obsession. Who was he and what was the obsession?

5. This Union general gained no distinction opposing

Ewell's raid on Washington. But he did achieve greater fame in writing *Ben Hur*. Who was he?

6. This ex-professor of Bowdoin College commanded a regiment at Gettysburg at Little Round Top and eventually rose to rank of brevet major general. He was later elected Governor of Maine. Who was he?

7. This man started the war as a private and finished as a lieutenant colonel. He saw action at Second Manassas, South Mountain, Antietam, Chancellorsville, Gettysburg, the Wilderness, Spotsylvania, and the Crater at Petersburg. He was also instrumental in the construction of the Brooklyn Bridge. Who was he?

8. This man was a prominent leader of the German-immigrant community. He was a Union general and had a park in New York City named after him. Who was he?

9. This woman, who followed the Union Army to care for wounded soldiers, later founded the American Red Cross. Who was she?

10. This Charleston woman was a noted diarist of the Civil War. Who was she?

11. This actress was the star of *Our American Cousin* and was performing the night Lincoln was shot. Who was she?

12. Born in Newark, this journalist wrote a novel about the Civil War in 1895 with vivid battle scenes learned entirely through research. Who was he? What was his book?

13. This father of a famous general rose to the rank of

brevet general in the Civil War. His military career took off following his impromptu charge up Missionary Ridge at Chattanooga. Who was he? Who was his son?

14. This Yankee inventor, who died prior to the Civil War, was responsible for two inventions that resulted in economic trends in the North and South which made the Civil War inevitable. Who was he? What were his inventions?

15. Which future president commanded a brigade in West Virginia?

16. This man, who was the second president to be assassinated, served in the war until 1863, when he was elected as a representative. Who was he?

17. This Confederate cavalry officer noted for his guerrilla exploits, later became U.S. consul to Hong Kong after the war. Who was he?

18. This Union general, who was a corps commander, was a major stockholder in the building of the Brooklyn Bridge. Who was he?

19. This union general, a corps commander at Gettysburg, ran against Garfield as the Democratic nominee in the 1880 election. Who was he?

20. This president did not fight in the Civil War. Instead, he "purchased" a substitute so that he could stay home and support his mother and sisters. He was the only president to serve nonconsecutive terms. Who was he?

Yes, there was a hit parade then. Although there were no Billboard Charts to list the popularity of these tunes, they did get around.

Songs

Which of the following songs were Confederate songs and which were Union:

1. "Lula Lula Lula is Gone"

2. "Virginia, Virginia, The Land of the Free"

3. "The Army Bean"

4. "Three Times Around She Went"

5. "Raw Recruit"

6. "Farewell to the Star-Spangled Banner"

7. "No Surrender"

8. "We Are the Boys of Potomac's Ranks"

9. "Maryland, My Maryland"

10. Which side did this rhyme belong to:

"Now I lay me down to sleep
In mud that's fathoms deep;
If I'm not here when you awake,
Just hunt me up with an oyster rake."

This nation's bloodiest war has also become a part of popular culture and literature. More people may be familiar with this than the minor details which fascinate historians and buffs.

Civil War in Books

1. What battle was the setting for *The Red Badge of Courage*?

2. What battle was the setting for *The Killer Angels*?

3. What novel written by a *New York Times* columnist deals with a young Confederate private? Who is the author?

4. Who wrote a biography of Robert E. Lee that won a Pulitzer Prize?

5. What past President of the United States dealt with the Civil War in his work *History of the American People*?

6. This short story about the Civil War was featured in an early issue of *Playboy* magazine. What was it? Who was it by?

7. Eugene O'Neill had a Civil War brigadier general as a character in one of his plays. Which one?

8. This British colonel of the Coldstream Guards observed part of the war from the Confederate side, and later wrote about his experience. Who was he?

9. Who wrote *Gone With the Wind*?

10. Who wrote the fictional history *If the South Had Won the Civil War*?

Civil War in Films

1. Name the silent epic about the Civil War directed by D. W. Griffith.

2. Name this Buster Keaton Civil War comedy, also of the silent-film era.

3. This Civil War film of the 1930s is notable because the first black to win an Oscar was in it. Name it.

4. This film starred John Wayne and Rock Hudson and concerned itself with the exploits of a group of Confederate diehards who flee to Mexico after the war. What was the name of this movie?

5. This John Wayne film dealt with the exploits of former Confederate cavalry officers fighting Indians in the West after the Civil War. What was the name of this movie?

6. Everybody knows that Clark Gable played Rhett Butler and Vivien Leigh played Scarlett O'Hara in *Gone with the Wind*. But who played the characters of Melanie Hamilton and Ashley Wilkes?

7. At what battle did Rhett Butler distinguish himself, even though this was not a scene in the film?

8. Who played the title role in *Young Mister Lincoln*?

9. What Civil War battle was featured in *How the West Was Won*?

10. This famous Spaghetti Western featured the Civil War as a backdrop for its actors, who included Clint Eastwood and Eli Wallach. What was it?

The Civil War on Television

1. Who played Abraham Lincoln in the TV miniseries *The Blue and the Gray*?

2. Who played Lincoln on the TV special "Sandburg's Lincoln"?

3. In the Walt Disney TV presentation "Willie and the

Yank,'' young Willie becomes attached to what famous Confederate military group?

4. Who played the part of Johnny Yuma in the TV series *The Rebel*?

5. Who provided the voice-over narration for *The Macahans*?

6. What was F Troops' Captain Parmenter's job during the Civil War?

7. In *The Twilight Zone* episode "The Passerby," who is the last person to walk down the "road to glory"?

8. In a famous sketch on *The Abbott and Costello Show*, where does Lou claim to have seen action while others were at Chickamauga?

9. On what TV series did an episode feature Abraham Lincoln fighting evil aliens on a far-off planet?

10. In the TV miniseries *Freedom Road*, who played the focal part of an ex-slave who rose to the position of U.S. Senator during Reconstruction?

ANSWERS

What Led to the War

1. $2 billion, or one half of all the combined southern states' wealth.

2. 385,000 out of a total white population of approximately 5.7 million.

3. Nat Turner.

4. South Carolina in 1828 wanted to leave the Union because of the high tariffs on foreign manufacturered goods.

5. He ordered federal troops into South Carolina.

6. In 1821 Congress admitted Missouri into the Union as a "slave state," even though previously slavery was not permitted north of a demarcation line.

7. 36°30′, North latitude.

8. 300,000.

9. The Fugitive Slave Act.

10. The change was to allow Territorial residents to decide whether they wanted to admit themselves in a "slave" or "free" state. The measure was introduced by Sen. Stephen Douglas of Illinois.

11. "Bushwackers" were pro-slavery people; "Jayhawkers" were "free-staters."

12. Kansas.

13. "Bleeding Kansas."

14. Pottawatamie Creek.

15. Dred Scott.

16. That his temporary residence in a free state where slavery was prohibited ended his slave status.

17. Chief Justice Roger Taney.

18. That Congress had no right to regulate slavery in territories and would only have that right if a congressional amendment was passed.

19. Justices McClean and Curtis.

20. An amendment required three-fourths of all the states' approval. Slave and free states were equal in number; therefore, an anti-slavery amendment could never pass.

21. Sen. Stephen A. Douglas and Abraham Lincoln.

22. It made Lincoln nationally known, and a contender for the Republican presidential nomination.

23. Virginia.

24. He was caught and hanged.

25. John Wilkes Booth.

Statistics

1. New York.

2. Oregon.

3. Virginia.

4. Florida.

5. Virginia.

6. New York.

7. Virginia.

8. 2.9 million.

9. 1.3 million.

10. The Union suffered approximately 385,000 killed and wounded. The Confederacy suffered about 329,000 killed and wounded.

Soldiers

Union

1. Officers had allowances to purchase their rations.

2. Hardtack.

3. A soldier with a constant run of bad luck.

4. A soldier who would always find a way of getting out of a detail.

5. A sewing kit furnished by a mother, sister, sweetheart, or the Soldier's Aid Society.

6. It was a list of offenders in a unit. It was referred to for assigning soldiers to disagreeable details.

7. Someone who enlisted for the bounty, or monetary bonus, and deserted the first chance he got.

8. A way for drill sergeants to teach "right" and "left" to people who did not know the meaning of those words. By tying a length of straw and hay to different legs, the soldier knew what direction to turn in when the drill sergeant said "hay foot" or "straw foot."

9. A civilian who made a living selling food or supplies to an army on the move.

10. A havelock is a piece of linen that hangs from the back of the cap over one's neck to protect it from the sun.

Confederate

1. A mixture of flour, water, and boiling bacon grease that was served as a ration after it cooled.

2. Farmer.

3. Two opponents would attack each other with hickory switches.

4. A cannonball.

5. A sport where cavalry riders would charge at and try to grab a gander tied just beyond their reach.

6. A game similar to "chicken."

7. A common form of punishment wherein the culprit wore a barrel with his crime labeled on it.

8. A sink.

9. The measles

10. Tea made from the bark of either slippery elm, sweet gum, willow, or dogwood.

Weapons

1. The percussion cap.

2. They had increased range and accuracy.

3. The minié ball—it had a conical appearance.

4. The Sharp's Carbine.

5. The Spencer Carbine.

6. The Henry Rifle.

7. Colt 1860 model.

8. Its shot balls were fired by percussion caps.

9. The "covered bridge" gun.

10. The Ager Coffee Mill Gun.

11. The Williams Machine Gun.

12. The Gatling Gun.

13. Its inventor, Dr. Richard R. Gatling, was a southern sympathizer, and as a result his invention was suspect.

14. .58 inch.

15. Seven.

16. In the stock.

17. Whitworths.

18. Enfields; .577.

19. A Quaker gun is a log painted black. At a distance it resembled a cannon. They were used at Confederate encampments at Manassas to fool the Union into thinking that the Confederate artillery was greater than it really was.

20. It was called canister shot, and was a can filled with "bad" balls. When fired, it had the effect of a giant shotgun shell.

Regiments and Units

1. The Iron Brigade.

2. 2nd Wisconsin, 6th Wisconsin, 7th Wisconsin, 19th Indiana, and 24th Michigan.

3. First Kentucky Confederate.

4. 2nd Kentucky, 4th Kentucky, 5th Kentucky, 6th Kentucky, 9th Kentucky.

5. Michigan Cavalry Brigade; 1st Michigan Cavalry, 5th Michigan Cavalry, 6th Michigan Cavalry, 7th Michigan Cavalry.

6. 1st Vermont Cavalry and 25th New York Cavalry.

7. Cavalry.

8. Officers judged to be less than satisfactory.

9. 1st Kansas Volunteer Cavalry.

10. 7th Kansas Cavalry; Jennison's Jayhawkers.

11. 2nd, 4th, 5th, 27th, and 33rd regiments of Virginia.

Politics of 1860

1. The Cooper Institute.

2. Chicago; the Wigwam.

3. Charleston, South Carolina.

4. Three.

5. William H. Seward.

6. Fifty-seven ballots were cast but no delegates were selected.

7. Stephen A. Douglas of Illinois with running mate Benjamin Fitzpatrick of Alabama.

8. John C. Breckinridge of Kentucky with Joseph Lane of Oregon.

9. Herschel Johnson of Georgia.

10. The party was made up of leftover Whigs. It was strongest in the border states.

11. John Bell with Edward Everett.

12. Lincoln—1.9 million; Douglas—1.4 million; Breckinridge—854,000; and Bell—591,000.

13. Lincoln—180; Breckinridge—72; Bell—39; Douglas—12.

14. Won Missouri, and partial electoral vote in New York.

15. Enthusiastic Lincoln supporters who held nighttime rallies by torchlight.

16. No.

17. Six states; 38 delegates.

18. One per state delegation.

19. Howell Cobb of Georgia.

20. Montgomery, Alabama.

21. One six-year term.

22. No.

23. No.

24. He could veto individual items in appropriations bills without having to veto the bill. This was called a line-item veto.

25. Two thirds.

Abraham Lincoln (1809–1865)

1. Hardin County, Kentucky.

2. Lincoln was 8 years old when his family moved to Indiana.

3. Nancy Hanks was his natural mother; Sally Bush was his stepmother.

4. *The Statutes of Indiana*.

5. The Black Hawk War of 1832. (A minor Indian war.)

6. Captain of the local militia.

7. Private . . . term of enlistment was thirty days.

8. State legislature for the Whig Party.

9. New Salem.

10. Out of eight candidates, he finished third, with 657 votes.

11. John T. Stuart.

12. 1834.

13. Anne Rutledge. She died of fever.

14. Mary Owens. She turned Lincoln down.

15. It was a resolution securing to the state a part of the proceeds of the sale of public lands within its limits. The resolution was tabled.

16. Committee of Public Accounts and Expenditures.

17. John T. Stuart.

18. Stephen A. Douglas.

19. Lincoln failed to show up for the wedding (they were finally married in 1842).

20. Henry Clay, who lost to James K. Polk.

21. He was elected to Congress. He was the only Whig in his state's delegation.

22. Until 1848.

23. Oregon. Lincoln turned down the offer when his wife refused it.

24. Lyman Trumbull.

25. The three parties were Democratic, Know Nothing, and Republican. Lincoln chose the Republican Party.

Jefferson Davis (1808–1889)

1. The American Revolution.

2. Christian County, Kentucky. He was less than a hundred miles from where Lincoln was born.

3. College of St. Thomas Aquinas. Davis was the only Protestant in a Catholic school.

4. Visiting a Tavern.

5. Participated in a Christmas Eve eggnog party with several other cadets.

6. Davis graduated 23rd in a class of 32.

7. Col. Zachary Taylor. His daughter's name was Sarah.

8. Conduct subversive to military discipline. Davis refused to answer reveille on a rainy morning.

9. His defense was that he had pneumonia and that he was resentful of Major Mason's harsh language, which Mason had used while addressing Davis in front of his company. Davis was acquitted.

10. Davis resigned to marry Sarah Taylor since her father did not want his daughter marrying an army officer.

11. Davis and his wife contracted malaria. She died.

12. Varina Howell.

13. Brierfield.

14. Davis belonged to the Democratic Party. He attended the Democratic convention at Jackson, going there as a delegate from Warren County.

15. He was nominated to run for a seat in the lower house of the state legislature, but a Whig beat him in the general election.

16. Congressman from Mississippi.

17. He was taking a stand against the Native American Party, and he opposed any measure that would be brought against immigrants that was then believed to be a way of "purifying the ballot box."

18. He favored the Mexican War.

19. Davis broke "the freshman rule," which expects a congressman to remain silent in his first term of office.

20. The 1st Mississippi Rifles. Davis was elected colonel.

21. Zachary Taylor.

22. Battle of Buena Vista.

23. Senator.

24. Military Affairs Committee.

25. Secretary of War.

Ulysses S. Grant (1822–1885)

1. Hiram Ulysses Grant.

2. Grant showed an early talent as an equestrian.

3. Grant was 17 when he entered West Point in 1839.

4. Sergeant of Battalion.

5. Grant was graduated 21st in a class of 35.

6. He was assigned to the 2nd Regiment.

7. He first saw action in Palo Alto.

8. Gen. Zachary Taylor.

9. 4th Regiment.

10. Quartermaster.

11. Chapultepec.

12. Fort Dallas, Oregon Territory.

13. Julia Dent.

14. 1854.

15. He worked as a dealer in the family leather goods store.

16. Given the rank of colonel, he was assigned to the 21st Illinois.

17. When four appointments for brigadier generalships came up for Illinois, Washburne made sure Grant got one of them.

18. Fremont appointed Grant to take command of Union Forces at Cairo, Ill.

19. "Unconditional Surrender," which matched his initials, U.S.

20. Horatio Seymour.

21. James A. Garfield.

22. Grant & Ward.

23. $450,000.

24. Full general (not used since George Washington held the rank).

25. Lieutenant general.

Robert E. Lee (1807–1870)

1. American Revolution.

2. 1828.

3. Joseph E. Johnston, who would later command the Army of Northern Virginia.

4. Lee graduated second in a class of 45.

5. General Winfield Scott.

6. The battle of Chapultepec.

7. Lee started the war as a captain, and ended it as a brevet colonel.

8. Lee was assigned to be the superintendent of West Point.

9. Mary Custis of Arlington.

10. Fitzhugh Lee, who would later serve under the Confederate cavalry general J.E.B. Stuart.

11. Second Cavalry Regiment, Lee was given the actual rank of lt. col. and served under Col. Albert Sydney Johnston.

12. Lee thought that slavery was evil, and an even greater evil for the white man.

13. Harpers Ferry.

14. The Union offered him the rank of full colonel, but the Confederacy offered him the rank of brigadier general.

15. Lee was offered command of an army of volunteers that would have between 75,000 and 100,000 men.

16. Commander of all forces in Virginia.

17. Brigadier general.

18. South Atlantic, which covered the southeastern coast. He held this command for ten months.

19. Davis appointed Lee to command the Army of Northern Virginia after Joseph Johnston was wounded.

20. "King of Spades," because he always had his men dig trenches and earthworks.

21. Traveler

22. Arming the slaves.

23. Richmond

24. Lee was writing for his pardon. He was placed in a category of Confederates that had to make individual applications for amnesty.

25. President of Washington College, Lexington, Va.

Braxton Bragg (1817–1876)

1. 1837.

2. Captain.

3. Seminole War.

4. Zachary Taylor.

5. Battle of Monterey.

6. "A little more grape, Captain Bragg." Taylor was referring to grapeshot.

7. Lieutenant colonel.

8. He was twice nearly assassinated, by whom he did not know.

9. A. S. Johnston.

10. He resigned from the army to run a plantation in Louisiana.

11. Commander-in-chief of all forces in Florida.

12. Brigadier general in charge of the garrison at Pensacola.

13. Santa Rosa.

14. Jefferson Davis' military adviser.

15. Command of forces at Wilmington, North Carolina.

16. As a capital military crime.

17. Firing into a flock of chickens during a move close to Union lines where stealth was required.

18. Retired to a plantation in Alabama.

19. 1,500 prisoners.

20. He was known as a general who could snatch defeat from the jaws of victory.

Thomas "Stonewall" Jackson
(1824–1863)

1. Someone else had withdrawn his application for West Point, thus creating a vacancy which Jackson sought.

2. "The Immortals," who were the lowliest group of cadets at West Point.

3. Jackson's lowest subject was Infantry Tactics, where he stood 21st in his class of 60.

4. Jackson misunderstood the colonel's orders, and marched the company off the parade ground and through the town.

5. K Company, 1st Artillery.

6. Siege of Vera Cruz.

7. An order to come to the rear.

8. They pursued the broken troops into Mexico City.

9. Major.

10. Virginia Military Institute (VMI)

11. Professor of Natural and Experimental Philosophy and Artillery Tactics.

12. He purchased six shares in the Bank of the Commonwealth of Virginia.

13. Tom Fool.

14. Jackson waited in the anteroom all night for Colonel Smith's return. "It never occurred to me to leave the spot of duty where my superior told me to stay," Jackson later said to Smith.

15. University of Virginia. Chairman of Mathematics. He had the recommendation of Col. Robert E. Lee.

16. Giving birth to his stillborn child.

17. Jackson was ordered to march the best cadets among the VMI upperclassmen to Richmond.

18. Jackson was made a colonel and ordered to Harpers Ferry.

19. Joseph Johnston.

20. First Battle of Manassas.

George McClellan (1826–1885)

1. 1842.

2. Philadelphia.

3. The minimum age regulation was waived since McClellan was only 15 upon entering West Point.

4. Future Union generals Foster, Reno, and Couch; and future Confederate generals Maury, D. R. Jones, W. D. Smith, Wilcox, Stonewall Jackson and George Pickett.

5. Fifth in a class of 60.

6. Brevet second lieutenant.

7. Vera Cruz.

8. McClellan had two horses shot out from under him, and was hit by some grapeshot.

9. Brevet captain.

10. Napoleon. He studied Napoleon's 1812 campaign.

11. Stonewall Jackson.

12. Exploring the sources of the Red River in Arkansas.

13. Nellie Marcy, the captain's daughter.

14. First Cavalry. Captain.

15. The Crimean War.

16. Chief engineer, Illinois Central Railroad.

17. Abraham Lincoln, counsel for the Illinois Central Railroad.

18. Vice-president.

19. Future Confederate general A. P. Hill.

20. A. P. Hill.

John Singleton Mosby (1833–1916)

1. Attorney.

2. Pro-Union.

3. Washington Mounted Rifles.

4. Private.

5. University of Virginia, Charlottesville.

6. Shooting the campus bully.

7. He was pardoned by the governor.

8. William J. Robertson.

9. Jeb Stuart.

10. Second New York.

11. A bullet creased his head.

12. Brigadier General Edwin H. Stoughton.

13. Captain.

14. Bradford Hoskins.

15. Maryland, because its citizens were not bound by conscription laws.

16. The chance to plunder.

17. The Partisan Ranger Act of 1862.

18. Fifth New York Cavalry Unit.

19. Forty-third Partisan Rangers.

20. Aide to Federal Governor of Virginia Colonel Dulaney.

William T. Sherman (1820–1891)

1. Cump. His brothers and sisters found his middle name, Tecumseh, too difficult to pronounce, so they shortened it.

2. 1836.

3. Benny Haven's was a grocery store. Sherman, along with other cadets, went there to purchase food to cook in their fireplaces, which was against regulations. He gained a reputation as the best hash-cooker at West Point, according to his classmate Thomas Rosecrans, a future Union general.

4. Sherman was assigned to the 3rd Artillery. It saw action in the Seminole War in Florida.

5. Sixth in a class of 43.

6. In that action, a column was dispatched while Sherman was under orders to stay behind in the fort.

7. A promotion to first lieutenant.

8. Fort Morgan, Mobile, Alabama.

9. In Pittsburgh on recruiting duty.

10. California—which was then a part of Mexico.

11. Sherman saw no action in the Mexican War. American troops had already seized California by the time he arrived.

12. The Gold Rush.

13. Selling common goods through a store in the area near the gold strike. Prices there were incredibly inflated, and Sherman made $2,000.

14. Eleanor Ewing. She was his childhood friend.

15. Sherman professed no religion.

16. Third Artillery, commanded by Captain Braxton Bragg.

17. Commissary Corps.

18. Banking. The firm was Lucas & Turner.

19. The day Sherman weathered a run on his bank.

20. Superintendent at a military academy in Alexandria, Louisiana.

"Jeb" Stuart (1833–1864)

1. "Jeb" was derived from his initials, J. E. B., which stood for James Ewell Brown.

2. War of 1812.

3. Thirteenth in a class of 46.

4. Cadet rank of cavalry sergeant.

5. Regiment of mounted riflemen in Texas; Brevet second lieutenant.

6. Second lieutenant in the 1st Cavalry.

7. Kansas.

8. John Brown.

9. A saber attachment.

10. Lt. Col. Robert E. Lee.

11. His promotion to captain.

12. Lieutenant Colonel of Infantry.

13. Col. T. J. "Stonewall" Jackson.

14. Colonel of Cavalry.

15. Brigadier general.

16. He rode toward them and ordered them to pull down a fence, put down their arms, and march through to the woods behind him where there were Confederate troops. The Union troops obeyed, thinking he was one of their officers.

17. 15th Pennsylvania Volunteers.

18. A very "short and retiring" chin.

19. "Beauty."

20. Battle of the Wilderness; at Yellow Tavern.

Other Union Generals

1. Maj. Gen. George Thomas.

2. All three of these northern military leaders were southern born.

3. McPherson graduated first in his class.

4. Hood graduated 44th in this class.

5. Henry W. Halleck.

6. Second Michigan Cavalry.

7. Napoleon and Frederick the Great.

8. Sheridan charged a cadet officer with a lowered bayonet after he thought the cadet gave him an improper order.

9. Sheridan was suspended for a year.

10. Jerome Napoleon Bonaparte, grandson of Napoleon's youngest brother.

11. Governor of Massachusetts.

12. Running mate in 1864.

13. Democratic.

14. Stephen Douglas.

15. Butler voted for Jefferson Davis fifty-seven times!

Other Confederate Generals

1. Patrick Henry, who was her uncle.

2. "He has the unfortunate knack of getting himself shot in nearly every engagement."

3. Army of the Shenandoah.

4. He was struck by a shell fragment and a minié ball.

5. William T. Sherman.

6. First Artillery.

7. Thirteenth Virginia Volunteers.

8. Chancellorsville.

9. Petersburg

10. Fourth Regiment.

11. Longstreet was a major and a paymaster.

12. A brigade.

13. "Old Pete"

14. Braxton Bragg

15. Battle of the Wilderness.

Abolitionists

1. *Uncle Tom's Cabin*, by Harriet Beecher Stowe.

2. Plymouth Church.

3. Rev. Henry Ward Beecher.

4. Liberty Party.

5. Free Soil Party.

6. Radical Abolition Party.

7. Douglass was reluctant to support Lincoln because, in 1860, Lincoln was not against slavery in slave states and did not oppose the Fugitive Slave Act.

8. Susan B. Anthony.

9. 400,000.

10. A federal project undertaken in 1862 where ten thousand slaves already abandoned by their masters were given government aid to build their own community.

Underground Railroad

1. A network of abolitionists who helped runaway slaves get to Canada.

2. The routes running from Kentucky to Ohio.

3. Harriet Tubman.

4. Maryland.

5. Salmon P. Chase.

6. Fugitive Slave Law, passed in February 1793.

7. Levi Coffin.

8. The Golden Rule and the Preamble to the Declaration of Independence.

9. Oberlin College.

10. The fourth and last time the legislature tried to repeal Oberlin's charter was in 1843. The vote was 36 to 29 against repeal.

Politics during the War—Union

1. Habeus Corpus.

2. William Seward, Secretary of State; Salmon P. Chase, Secretary of the Treasury; Edward Bates, Attorney General; Montgomery Blair, Postmaster General; Gideon Welles, Secretary of the Navy; Simon Cameron, Secretary of War.

3. Issuance of the Emancipation Proclamation.

4. Salmon P. Chase.

5. Minister to Russia.

6. Edwin M. Stanton.

7. England.

8. Andrew Johnson.

9. Charles Francis Adams.

10. New York City.

11. George McClellan.

Politics during the War—Confederate

1. Montgomery, Alabama.

2. The Alabama delegation objected to the move.

3. Granville H. Oury.

4. Alexander H. Stephens.

5. Robert Toombs, Secretary of State; Christopher Memminger, Secretary of the Treasury; Leroy Pope Walker, Secretary of War; Stephen Russell Mallory, Secretary of the Navy; John H. Regan, Postmaster General; Judah P. Benjamin, Attorney General.

6. Virginia, North Carolina, Alabama, Florida and Tennessee.

7. $100 to $5,000.

8. 315 regiments and 58 battalions.

9. It drafted all males between the ages of 16 and 60, with those between the ages of 18 and 45 eligible for field service.

10. Slightly over 40 percent.

Fort Sumter

1. Maj. Robert Anderson.

2. *Powhatan, Pocahontas, Baltic,* and revenue cutter *Harriet Lane.*

3. Pensacola.

4. P. G. T. Beauregard.

5. First Artillery.

6. Fifteen commissioned officers, 74 enlisted men, 1 mail carrier, and 43 civilian employees.

7. At 4:30 A.M., April 12, 1861.

8. Lt. Henry S. Farley, a Confederate. (Though this has been subject to debate).

9. The 87th Regiment.

10. April 15.

11. Abner Doubleday

12. *Pawnee, Harriet Lane,* and chartered liner *Baltic.*

13. Doubleday, at 7:30 A.M., at a Confederate ironclad battery on Cummings Point on Morris Island.

14. Seven hundred.

15. He set up a continuous watch, since an assault was feared.

16. Fort Moultrie.

17. Three hundred.

18. Col. Louis Wigfall.

19. Nearly forty thousand.

20. Pvt. Daniel Hough

Naval War

1. *C.S.S. Virginia; U.S.S. Merrimack*

2. The Monitor was built in Brooklyn.

3. Matthew Fontaine Maury.

4. Stephen Russell Mallory. . . . He was a senator from Florida assigned to the senate's naval committee.

5. Comdr. Franklin Buchanan.

6. The *Congress* and the *Cumberland*.

7. John Ericsson.

8. John L. Worden.

9. Two 11-inch Dahlgren guns.

10. Catesby Jones.

11. *C.S.S. Tennessee*.

12. The *U.S.S. Hartford;* Adm. David Farragut.

13. A series of twenty-three ships the Union ordered built at the war's beginning. They got their name because they were all built in less than four months.

14. A torpedo boat was a cigar-shaped, steam-powered boat about fifty feet long. It carried a torpedo on a long boom mounted on the bow.

15. A torpedo in those days was a canister of gunpowder placed against a ship's hull and detonated. They could also be moored. (They are known today as mines.)

16. Capt. Charles Wilkes.

17. *C.S.S. Manassas*.

18. The *Carondelet*, the *St. Louis*, the *Cincinatti*, and the *Essex*.

19. Flag officer Andrew Foote.

20. That every shot cost the Union eight dollars and that he didn't want any shots wasted.

21. The *Carondelet*.

22. *C.S.S. Arkansas;* Yazoo City.

23. Vicksburg.

24. *C.S.S. Chicora; C.S.S. Palmetto State.*

25. Lifting the blockade of Charleston in 1863.

26. Adm. Samuel DuPont.

27. *The Weehawken, Passaic, Montauk, Patapsco, New Ironsides, Catskill, Nantucket, Nahant* and *Keokuk.*

28. It was the blockade runner that brought in the largest military cargo for the Confederacy during the war.

29. It couldn't get back to England because the Union blockade was too tight.

30. The Confederacy bought the *Fingal* and converted it into the ironclad *C.S.S. Atlanta.*

31. The *Weehawken* and the *Nahant.*

32. The pilothouse was located on top of the turret.

33. Cheesebox on a raft; tin can on a shingle.

34. Foote was sent to replace DuPont, but died. He was replaced by Adm. John Dahlgren.

35. The *U.S.S. New Ironsides.*

36. The *C.S.S. Hunley* fought for the Confederacy, and sank the *U.S.S. Housatonic.*

37. The *C.S.S. Albermarle.*

38. Plymouth.

39. *Miami* and *Southfield.*

40. Lt. William Cushing.

41. He sank the *Albermarle* by sailing a steam cutter to the ironclad and exploding a torpedo next to its hull.

42. *Oreto*, renamed *C.S.S. Florida*.

43. The *C.S.S. Florida* was captured in Bahia, Brazil, by the *U.S.S. Wachusett*. The capture of the *Florida* violated Brazil's neutrality in the Civil War, which is considered a breach of international law.

44. *Enrica*, renamed *C.S.S. Alabama*.

45. Raphael Semmes.

46. John Maffit.

47. *U.S.S. Hatteras*.

48. Antwerp.

49. Capt. John A. Winslow.

50. *The Kearsage*.

51. *C.S.S. Shenandoah*.

Shenandoah Valley, 1862

1. 3,600.

2. General Banks; Kenrstown.

3. Banks 9,000; Jackson 3,000; Banks.

4. McClellan.

5. John C. Fremont.

6. McDowell's Corps.

7. No. 199.

8. 8,500 infantry, 1,000 cavalry.

9. Milroy; Frémont's.

10. "Foot cavalry."

11. Virginia Military Institute (V.M.I.).

12. Ewell's.

13. Col. James Walker—13th Virginia.

14. Maj. Roberdeau Chatham Wheat.

15. Front Royal.

16. Nathaniel Banks'.

17. Cross Keys.

18. Port Republic.

19. Three.

20. 60,000.

Peninsular Campaign—Spring, 1862

1. Port Urbana on the Rappahannock River.

2. York Peninsula.

3. McDowell's Corps.

4. Fifty-six.

5. The Chickahominy River.

6. The observation balloon; Prof. T. S. C. Lowe.

7. The Battle of Fair Oaks.

8. General Joseph Johnston.

9. Robert E. Lee.

10. Keyes' Corps.

11. Ambrose P. Hill & J. B. Magruder.

12. Jeb Stuart.

13. The Seven Days.

14. Mechanicsville.

15. Gaines Mill.

16. York to James.

17. Battle of Frayser's Farm.

18. Battle of Malvern Hill.

19. Hill's and Magruder's.

20. Lincoln offered to send fifty thousand men. McClellan said it would not be enough to take Richmond.

Red River Campaign

1. Texas.

2. Cotton.

3. N. P. Banks.

4. *Black Hawk*.

5. Fort Humbug.

6. Henderson's Hill.

7. The Red River failed to rise.

8. The *Eastport*.

9. Col. Augustus Buchel.

10. Saline Crossroads.

Sherman's Advance toward Atlanta and the Subsequent Battles for Atlanta

1. General Johnston; Corps Comdr. William J. Hardee and John B. Hood.

2. Army of the Cumberland—Major General Thomas; Army of Tennessee—Maj. Gen. James B. McPherson; Army of Ohio—Maj. Gen. John M. Schofield.

3. Rocky Face Ridge.

4. McPherson's.

5. Four thousand.

6. The Army of the Mississippi—Major General Polk.

7. The Union army crossed to his rear on the Oostanaula River.

8. The Battle of Kennesaw Mountain.

9. Roswell.

10. July 17, 1864.

11. Gen. John B. Hood.

12. Sixty thousand Confederate facing a hundred thousand Union.

13. Peachtree Creek; 5,000.

14. General Hardee.

15. General McPherson.

16. O. O. Howard.

17. Ezra Church; July 28, 1864; Howard fought Confederate Corps of Stephen, Lee, and Stewart.

18. Joe Wheeler's.

19. August 31, 1864; Jonesboro.

20. September 1, 1864.

Sherman's March to the Sea

1. John B. Hood.

2. Two.

3. Henry Slocum and Oliver O. Howard.

4. November 15.

5. Forage "liberally."

6. $100,000,000.

7. One-fifth useful and four-fifths waste.

8. General Hardee; 10,000.

9. Fort McAllister.

10. Outside of Macon.

Hood's Winter Offensive

1. To make Sherman retreat from Georgia by striking at his supply route to the northwest and invade Tennessee.

2. Thirty-four thousand infantry and 12,000 cavalry.

3. General Slocum.

4. Four days.

5. Resaca. The Union forces refused to surrender, so Hood marched on.

6. He ripped up the railroad tracks to Atlanta and then marched to the sea to reestablish supply and communication on the Atlantic Coast.

7. Schofield's; Columbia, Tennessee.

8. Hood inexplicably let Schofield march past him and north to Franklin.

9. He planned to retire to Nashville for that night.

10. He ordered an immediate attack.

11. About 20,000.

12. About 6,500.

13. Twelve, of which six died.

14. About 24,000.

15. General Thomas.

16. About 55,000.

17. Two weeks.

18. Thomas attacked again the next day, thus shattering Hood's army.

19. About 18,000.

20. Tupelo, Mississippi.

Final Campaigns

1. Bermuda Hundred.

2. Ben Butler.

3. Richmond.

4. Fort Darling at Drewry's Bluff.

5. General P. G. T. Beauregard.

6. Hanover Junction.

7. Near Hanovertown.

8. Haw's Shop.

9. Cold Harbor.

10. Sixty thousand.

11. Eight minutes.

12. Eight thousand.

13. W. F. "Buddy" Smith's.

14. Dimmork Line.

15. Anderson's division.

16. Fifteen thousand.

17. A. P. Hill's.

18. Wright's Corps and Hancock's Corps (commanded by David Birney).

19. Jerusalem Plank Road.

20. A 500-foot-long mine tunnel.

Early's Raid

1. Franz Sigel's.

2. Two hundred thousand dollars was asked for; only twenty thousand was brought back.

3. Frederick.

4. Wright's corps.

5. Two thousand.

6. Lew Wallace.

7. Battle of Monocacy.

8. Fort Stevens.

9. Seventh Street Road.

10. White's Ford.

Quantrill's Raids

1. Johnston's.

2. George Todd.

3. They suffered a surprise attack from Company D, 1st Missouri Cavalry.

4. John Little and Ed Koger were killed. George Todd escaped.

5. Every able-bodied man had to enlist in the Union militia to get rid of guerrillas.

6. Independence.

7. Lone Jack.

8. Lawrence, Kansas.

9. It was the order to clear the border counties of civilians, thus depriving Quantrill of civilian support.

10. He lost an argument to Todd after accusing him of cheating at cards.

Morgan's Raids

1. Black Bess.

2. Lebanon.

3. Eight thousand dollars.

4. The 2nd Kentucky Cavalry.

5. Raiding the L & N Railroad at Gallatin.

Nathan Bedford Forrest's Raids

1. Shiloh.

2. Crittenden.

3. Cavalry Corps, Army of Tennessee.

4. One thousand seven hundred.

5. Colonel Straight.

First Manassas

1. Maj. Gen. Irwin McDowell.

2. Bull Run was a creek that ran through the Manassas battlefield.

3. McDowell's HQ was in Arlington, in Robert E. Lee's house.

4. The objective was Manassas Junction.

5. McDowell was in a hurry to do battle because the

ninety-day enlistments were soon to expire for many of his troops.

6. Gen. Robert Patterson. His army was to keep Confederate Gen. Joseph Johnston's forces pinned in the Shenandoah Valley.

7. Patterson had fought in the War of 1812 and the Mexican War.

8. Stonewall Jackson's rank was brigadier general.

9. The first skirmish was fought at Blackburn's Ford.

10. McDowell wanted to engage the Confederates on his left flank and keep them occupied while a large force tried to outflank them farther north from the Union right flank.

11. Sudley Springs.

12. S. P. Heintzelman and David Hunter.

13. Mrs. Judith Henry, at Henry House Hill.

14. Commanders Bee, Barton and Evans.

15. On Henry House Hill.

16. Tyler's.

17. William T. Sherman.

18. P. G. T. Beauregard.

19. Six senators and ten congressmen.

20. The 33rd Virginia.

Shiloh

1. It was the first big, bloody battle of the war.

2. Albert Sydney Johnston.

3. Grant was 39.

4. Both generals were experiencing difficulties with their superiors.

5. Corinth.

6. Grant commanded the Army of Tennessee, while Johnston commanded the Army of Mississippi.

7. Brig. Gen. William T. Sherman.

8. Braxton Bragg.

9. John C. Breckenridge.

10. The 25th Missouri Infantry for the Union; the 3rd Mississippi Battalion for the Confederates.

11. Jeff Davis.

12. The Confederates outnumbered the Union: 40,000 to 35,000.

13. "We must this day conquer or perish."

14. The Orleans Guard Battalion, which was fired upon by the Confederates because they went into battle wearing blue uniforms.

15. The medical first was a field hospital tent that permitted the treatment of the wounded on the battlefield.

16. The Hornet's Nest.

17. A bayonet charge.

18. In the leg.

19. The Ninth Illinois, which suffered 59-percent casualties.

20. The Army of Ohio, Commanded by Don Carlos Buell.

Second Manassas

1. Maj. Gen. John Pope.

2. Federal Army of Virginia.

3. Fighting in the Peninsular Campaign.

4. Franz Sigel attacked Jackson's corps.

5. Fitz-John Porter.

6. Longstreet's corps.

7. The Peninsular Campaign.

8. An unfinished railroad cut.

9. Henry House Hill.

10. Sixteen thousand Union, 9,000 Confederate.

•

Antietam

1. Jackson captured Harpers Ferry, and eleven thousand Union troops.

2. Sharpsburg, Maryland.

3. Lee was outnumbered two to one.

4. It had the bloodiest single day's fight in the Civil War.

5. McClellan wanted to hit hard at both flanks of the Confederate army to draw their units from the center to reinforce their flanks. Then he was to commit his reserves to hitting the weakened center of the Confederate line.

6. Joseph Hooker.

7. Dunker Church.

8. Hood and D. H. Hill.

9. Hooker took a ball in the foot.

10. Bloody Lane.

11. Ambrose Burnside.

12. Antietam Creek.

13. The Burnside Bridge.

14. Brig. Gen. Robert Toombs, who had two regiments of Georgia infantry.

15. Miller's Farm.

16. A. P. Hill's division.

17. Hill's division marched from Harpers Ferry, seventeen miles away.

18. McClellan lost twelve thousand men.

19. Lee lost nine thousand men.

20. The Emancipation Proclamation.

Fredericksburg

1. Ambrose Burnside commanded the Union Army; Lee commanded the Confederate Army.

2. Only five hundred troops.

3. One day's march away in Culpeper.

4. Pontoon bridges.

5. Commander-in-Chief Halleck.

6. Foggy.

7. Stonewall Jackson.

8. Longstreet.

9. One hundred feet.

10. Joseph Hooker.

11. Hooker protested the orders to Burnside, but finally obeyed them.

12. William Franklin.

13. He sent 4,500 men, or one division.

14. George Gordon Meade.

15. A gap in the Confederate line.

16. Jackson counterattacked and drove Meade back.

17. The Union lost twelve thousand men; the Confederates lost five thousand men.

18. Maj. John Pelham.

19. Two guns (or cannons).

20. Pennsylvania.

Murfreesboro

1. The Battle of Stones River.

2. Maj. Gen. William Rosecrans.

3. Nashville.

4. "Old Rosey."

5. Sheridan's division.

6. The Round Forest.

7. Brig. Gen. James R. Chalmers

8. "Hell's Half-Acre."

9. William B. Hazen's.

10. Both armies did not fight, but held their positions.

11. Rosecrans dispatched a division to take a hill across Stones River to the east.

12. The division came from Crittenden's Corps.

13. Breckinridge protested Bragg's order.

14. The Confederates won the battle for the hill.

15. The massed fire of fifty-eight Union guns forced the Confederates to give up the hill.

16. The Confederates lost twelve thousand men, while the Union lost thirteen thousand men.

17. One-third of the Union army was either AWOL or in the hospital.

18. Stage an offensive or be replaced.

19. "Sandy fellows."

20. Muster the officers out of the army.

Chancellorsville

1. General Joseph Hooker.

2. Hooker wanted to trap Lee between two columns of his army. Each wing would have 60,000 men—equal in strength to Lee's army. The two wings would converge on Lee from Fredericksburg in the east and Morrisville in the west.

3. John Sedgwick.

4. Anderson's division.

5. Pleasonton managed to obtain a Confederate officer's diary.

6. An account of a March meeting between Confederate

commanders Jackson, A. P. Hill, Ewell and Stuart deciding that the next battle would be at Chancellorsville.

7. Night of May 1, when Lee and Jackson met and talked about the possibility of turning the Union flank.

8. Word from Jeb Stuart's cavalry on the disposition of the Union line.

9. That the Union right flank did not extend northward to the Rappahannock River where it would have been safely anchored.

10. Jubal Early.

11. "Fighting Joe."

12. Dividing his already small army in the face of a numerically superior Union army.

13. At 4:00 A.M.

14. 31,700.

15. 12,900.

16. 70,000.

17. Daniel Sickles, III Corps.

18. The Wilderness.

19. The prisoners told him that they were marching to turn the Union right flank. Sickles thought they were lying, and believed Lee was retreating.

20. Maj. Gen. O. O. Howard. He only had one arm, having lost the other at the battle of Fair Oaks.

21. The XI Corps was held in the lowest esteem by the Army of the Potomac because it comprised mostly Germans.

22. The corps was overrun by surprise by Jackson's corps.

23. A. P. Hill.

24. He was shot accidentally by his own troops.

25. Jeb Stuart.

Vicksburg

1. "Vicksburg is the key. The war can be brought to a close if the key is in our pocket."

2. It was a rail point that received Confederate supplies and goods coming down the Red, White and Arkansas Rivers.

3. John C. Pemberton. He was the only northern-born Confederate general who achieved rank of lieutenant general.

4. John A. McClernand.

5. The plan was to give McClernand's Army to Sherman before McClernand could take command.

6. The successful capture of Fort Hindman.

7. Chickasaw Bluffs. Union suffered 1,800 casualties, while the Confederates lost only 187 men.

8. McClernand, Sherman, and James McPherson.

9. From the east, or landward, side.

10. Milliken's Bend.

11. Grant tried to have his men dig a canal across the DeSoto Peninsula, which lies across the river from Vicksburg.

12. The venture was not a success. The river's water level receded during construction of the canal, making it useless.

13. Fifteen miles.

14. Fort Pemberton.

15. Hard Times.

16. The flotilla had to make a dash downriver under the guns emplaced in the heights around Vicksburg.

17. Pemberton wanted to send three brigades, or eight thousand men, to Bragg.

18. Pemberton finally sent Bragg two brigades.

19. The Union had to silence the Confederate battery at Grand Gulf.

20. Port Hudson.

21. Bruinsburg.

22. Col. B. F. Grierson. He was a bandmaster before the war.

23. Jackson, Mississippi.

24. E. O. C. Ord.

25. Grant had the captured Confederates paroled.

Gettysburg

1. Major General Reynolds.

2. Gen. Abner Doubleday.

3. I, III, and XI Corps.

4. Maj. Gen. George Gordon Meade.

5. I Corps, Lt. Gen. James Longstreet; II Corps, Lt.
   Gen. Richard Ewell; III Corps, Lt. Gen A. P. Hill;
   Cavalry Corps, Maj. Gen. J. E. B. Stuart.

6. Heth's division for the Confederacy; Buford's cavalry
   division for the Union.

7. Little Round Top was a hill that overlooked the
   battlefield which had a clear and complete view of the
   entire action. Its commanding view made it an excel-
   lent artillery position.

8. Lee ordered his army to hit both Union flanks.

9. Longstreet wanted to circle around the Union left
   flank and hit the Yankees from the rear.

10. Lee did not want to risk this move because he had no cavalry to find out what was the disposition of the Union army.

11. Maj. Gen. Henry Slocum's XII Corps at Culp's Hill.

12. The 20th Maine.

13. A. P. Hill's.

14. Devil's Den.

15. The Wheatfield and the Peach Orchard.

16. Smash the Union center.

17. Pickett's division.

18. Seminary Ridge.

19. Pettigrew's and Trimble's Divisions.

20. It had done the most marching and seen the least action for the previous year.

21. Virginia.

22. The 13th and 16th Vermont.

23. The 8th Ohio.

24. Conf. Brig. Gen. Louis Armistead; Maj. Gen. Winfield Scott Hancock.

25. 1,500; 4,500.

Chickamauga

1. Longstreet's corps.

2. Both the Union and Confederate armies were roughly equal in number. In many of the major battles, the Union outnumbered the Confederates.

3. Polk was an Episcopal bishop.

4. Destroy the Union army piecemeal, since it was advancing into Georgia in separate corps.

5. Forrest's cavalry division attacked a Union division from Thomas' corps at Reed's Bridge.

6. Bragg's objective was the Lafayette Road, which led back to the Union base in Chattanooga.

7. McCook's Corps.

8. Longstreet commanded the left; Polk commanded the right.

9. Polk would strike Thomas' corps first. Longstreet would then launch his attack once he saw Polk making progress.

10. The delay permitted Rosecrans to reinforce Thomas.

11. Breckinridge's men.

12. Thomas J. Wood's division.

13. The movement opened a hole in the Union line which Longstreet saw as the perfect opportunity to attack.

14. The Union line collapsed and retreated.

15. Rosecrans left for Chattanooga to plan a last stand.

16. Thomas pulled in his line around Snodgrass Hill.

17. Maj. Gen. Gordon Granger.

18. Retreat to Chattanooga.

19. Longstreet wanted to pursue the beaten army, but Bragg was not convinced that this should be done.

20. Eighteen thousand Confederates were lost, vs. 16,000 Union.

Chattanooga

1. Lookout Mountain.

2. Missionary Ridge.

3. Maj. Gen Joseph Hooker.

4. Maj. Gen. George Thomas.

5. The Union army was cut off from its supply line.

6. Hooker's corps reestablished the supply line. The position was called "The Cracker Line."

7. Brown's Ferry, which was seized by a force commanded by Brig. Gen. W. F. "Baldy" Smith.

8. Sherman.

9. Custer L. Stevenson.

10. Longstreet.

11. Tunnel Hill.

12. Hardee, who replaced Polk.

13. Pat Cleburne.

14. Orchard Knob.

15. Thomas' men were to advance no farther than the Confederate trenches at the base of the ridge.

16. Sherman did not succeed in taking Tunnel Hill.

17. Thomas had four divisions.

18. Thomas' men charged up the ridge and pushed the Confederates back.

19. Dalton.

20. Cleburne's division.

Battle of the Wilderness and Spotsylvania

1. Hancock, Sedgwick and Warren.

2. What visibility? The dense underbrush and thick smoke from all the firing guns blinded most troops. Most soldiers hardly saw their enemies.

3. Lee wanted to personally lead the brigade into battle.

4. The brigade refused to advance until Lee went to the rear.

5. Sedgwick's corps.

6. Instead of retreating to the river crossing, Grant advanced south to Spotsylvania.

7. Lee's army got to Spotsylvania first.

8. Sedgwick.

9. Todd's Tavern.

10. Jubal Early.

11. The Mule Shoe.

12. Hancock's corps was sent to attack the Mule Shoe.

13. Gordon's division stopped the Union attack.

14. Gordon was successful in retaking the Mule Shoe.

15. Afterwards, it was called the Bloody Angle.

16. Wilderness Tavern.

17. Longstreet.

18. Two weeks.

19. The Union lost approximately 35,000 to the Confederate loss of 18,000.

20. The losses were a greater setback to Lee because he could not replace them.

Appomattox

1. Sheridan's.

2. Custer.

3. Auld Lang Syne.

4. 7,892.

5. 63.

6. 2,100.

7. The old days back during the Mexican War.

8. Officers and their men would be paroled and disqualified

from taking up arms until properly exchanged. All arms and ammunition and supplies were to be delivered as captured property.

9. Officers' side arms.

10. Private baggage and horses.

11. General Seth Williams, an acquaintance from Lee's days as superintendent at West Point.

12. About 25,000.

13. Grant, Meade, Hunt, Wilcox, Wise.

14. The pine table upon which the surrender was signed. It cost him twenty dollars in gold.

15. Gave it Custer as a gift for his wife.

16. Alexander. He suggested continued guerrilla warfare.

17. Lt. Col. Charles A. Whittier.

18. He took all the cavalry, determined not to surrender.

19. That conditions for surrender would not be any worse than Lee's imposing them himself.

20. Gordon's corps.

Andersonville

1. Georgia.

2. Twenty-five acres.

3. Thirty-five thousand.

4. A light railing which, when crossed by prisoners, would draw a shot from the sentries.

5. Sixty-four.

6. 24 12 lb. Napoleon Parrots.

7. Three-fourths of a pound bread or meal; one-eighth pound meat per day.

8. For a sewer.

9. Six acres.

10. About a hundred.

Lincoln's Assassination

1. Ford's Theater.

2. *Our American Cousin*.

3. Vice-President Andrew Johnson and Secretary of State William Seward.

4. John Wilkes Booth; he used a derringer.

5. Major Rathbone and Miss Harris.

6. Rathbone tried to stop Booth, but Booth stabbed him in the arm.

7. "Sic Semper Tyrranis," and "Revenge for the South."

8. "Wal, I guess I know enough to turn you inside out, you sockdologizing old mantrap!"

9. Booth broke his leg.

10. Lewis Paine.

11. David Herold.

12. In bed, recovering from a carriage accident.

13. Seward did survive the attack.

14. George Atzerodt.

15. Atzerodt did not go through with his attack, since he stopped at a bar to have a drink.

16. Petersen.

17. Secretary of War Edwin Stanton.

18. Stanton believed the plot to kill the president was broad-based; and that several hundred Confederate

terrorists were in Washington to slay other cabinet officials and burn the city.

19. Dr. Samuel Mudd.

20. Booth was cornered in a Virginia barn and shot by Federal troops. Atzerodt, Paine and Herold were all tried and hanged.

Reconstruction

1. White supremacists bent on opposing Republicanism in the South.

2. Arkansas, Louisiana, Tennessee, and Virginia.

3. All Confederate military and political leaders, and all Confederates worth over $20,000.

4. A convention to support Andrew Johnson's policies; August 1866, in Philadelphia; to form a political party that was neither Democratic nor Republican.

5. It was nicknamed the arm-in-arm convention because delegates from Massachusetts and North Carolina entered the hall arm in arm.

6. West Virginia, Missouri, and Tennessee.

7. Delaware, Maryland, and Kentucky.

8. Republican—129; Democrats—35.

9. *Ex Parte Milligan.*

10. It forbade the organization of militias in ten Southern states unless they were authorized by Congress.

11. It instructed commanders in the South to arrest persons charged in violent acts where civil authorities had not acted, and to hold them until a proper court could try them.

12. U. S. Grant.

13. General Sheridan; Gen. George Thomas.

14. Winfield Scott Hancock—who accepted the position after it was declined by Thomas.'

15. Ratification of the Fourteenth Amendment and Negro suffrage.

16. Nathan Bedford Forrest; Robert E. Lee.

17. Each state was a realm, ruled by a Grand Dragon.

18. The Invisible Empire.

19. Nashville.

20. William Woods Holden, North Carolina, 1871.

Quotations

1. Maj. Gen. George Gordon Meade at Fredericksburg.

2. Gen. Robert E. Lee at Fredericksburg.

3. William T. Sherman, on his March to the Sea.

4. Adm. David Farragut at Mobile Bay.

5. Abraham Lincoln, from his Gettysburg Address.

6. Abraham Lincoln, from his Second Inaugural Address.

7. Abraham Lincoln, on the fall of Vicksburg.

8. Robert E. Lee, on his acceptance of the presidency of Washington College.

9. Stonewall Jackson's last words.

10. Lt. Gen. James Longstreet's comments to a Pennsylvania woman whose pigs and cows were "requisitioned" by the Confederate Army.

11. J. E. B. Stuart's last words.

12. Jefferson Davis, addressing Hood's army before the invasion of Tennessee in 1864.

13. Lt. Gen. John Bell Hood's address to his troops before the invasion of Tennessee in 1864.

14. Sheridan telegraphing Grant on pursuit of Lee's army.

15. Lee's Farewell To His Troops.

16. Berry Benson.

17. Confederate general Edmund Kirby-Smith.

18. McClellan writing to Grant.

19. Maj. Gen. George "Pap" Thomas.

20. U. S. Grant.

Famous People during the War

1. Edwin Booth (brother of John Wilkes Booth).

2. George Armstrong Custer.

3. Matthew Brady.

4. Abner Doubleday—baseball.

5. Lew Wallace.

6. Joshua Lawrence Chamberlain.

7. Washington Roebling.

8. Carl Schurz.

9. Clara Barton.

10. Mary Chesnut.

11. Laura Keene.

12. *The Red Badge of Courage*, by Stephen Crane.

13. Lt. Gen. Arthur MacArthur. His son was five-star general Douglas MacArthur.

14. Eli Whitney: his cotton gin, which removed seeds from cotton thus making it more profitable to grow. His other invention was the implementing of interchangeable parts, thus making mass production possible.

15. Rutherford B. Hayes.

16. James A. Garfield.

17. John Singleton Mosby.

18. Henry Slocum.

19. Winfield Scott Hancock.

20. Grover Cleveland.

Songs

1. Confederate.

2. Confederate.

3. Union.

4. Confederate.

5. Union.

6. Confederate.

7. Confederate.

8. Union.

9. Confederate.

10. Union.

Civil War in Books

1. Chancellorsville.

2. Gettysburg.

3. *Unto This Hour,* by Tom Wicker.

4. Douglas Southall Freeman.

5. Woodrow Wilson.

6. "An Occurrence at Owl Creek Bridge," by Ambrose Bierce.

7. *Mourning Becomes Electra.*

8. Colonel Fremantle.

9. Margaret Mitchell.

10. MacKinley Kantor.

Civil War in Films

1. *Birth of a Nation.*

2. *The General.*

3. *Gone with the Wind.*

4. *The Undefeated.*

5. *She Wore a Yellow Ribbon.*

6. Olivia De Havilland and Leslie Howard.

7. The Battle of Franklin.

8. Henry Fonda.

9. Shiloh.

10. *The Good, The Bad, and The Ugly.*

The Civil War on Television

1. Gregory Peck.

2. Hal Holbrook.

3. Mosby's Raiders.

4. Nick Adams.

5. William Conrad.

6. The officers' laundry.

7. Abraham Lincoln.

8. Chicadee ("You were at Chickamauga, I was at Chickadee").

9. *Star Trek.*

10. Muhammad Ali.